How to Brand Yourself for your Network Marketing Business

9 Simple Steps to Explode your Business Using Easy, Simple Methods Online

David Williams

How to Brand Yourself for your Network Marketing Business

ISBN 978-1505286762

Table of Contents

A complete Reversal from Everything You Thought You Knew

Before we get into the nitty-gritty, I want to remind you what this book is NOT about:

-It's NOT about spending endless hours on Facebook, Twitter, or any other time vampires

-It's NOT for anyone except Network Marketers – Hey, if you're not in our industry, you're welcome to read this book, but it's not going to work for you at all if you're not a networker

-It's NOT about the typical methods that personal branding sites all preach – because they are NOT for networkers. Our industry is different; it's NOT Internet Marketing, it's NOT Traditional Marketing or SEO, so if you are not one of 'us' forget this book, or just pass it to someone who is a networker...

However....

If you are one of 'us' and want to find a way to close more business, to have more clout with cold market, if you want to stop sponsor-shoppers, and to close your prospects without the need of your upline, if you want to be more confident because your prospect is pre-sold on you, then this is YOUR BOOK!

Welcome to all the shortcuts, insider branding methods, and Internet secrets for pre-qualifying prospects that all the big names use, and you can too.

Once again, I'm spilling the beans that your upline paid thousands to learn... and you now own for less than 20 bucks.

And unlike seminars, you're welcomed and encouraged to email me if you have any question or want any guidance. I'd also like it if you just dropped me a line telling me you have this book, and what program you are promoting.

David Williams davidwilliamsauthor@gmail.com

The first thing to learn is this….

YOU are the brand, and YOU are the expert. Not your product and not your company.

I know this flies in the face of traditional marketing, or even online marketing of products. Network Marketing is different. YOU are looking to attract prospects and to build YOUR downline. This is what you bring to your company, so it is YOU that is the lynchpin.

You will often hear your upline tell you, 'It's the same products, the same comp plan for each of us,' the lesson being that if things don't go well, it's not the product, or the company, or the comp plan at fault (it's your fault). At the same time, if you are successful, it's also because of you. So, YOU are the key ingredient for success in MLM.

Funny thing, the same people who do these trainings, saying '…the only difference is you…' meaning if you don't succeed it's your responsibility (which I do believe is true), will also dance across the stage at a company event, and when asked about their success, thank everyone from the company president down to the last clerk in Distributor services, and all the people who invented the product, instead of being consistent and saying 'It was plain old hard work and smart work that made it possible for me to reach this position.' The "thank everyone' Academy Award kind of testimony does nothing for new people in the audience listening – when they hear this sort of testimony, they think 'this is just like my corporate job – you have to kiss butt to succeed.' So don't do it.

Your success is not based on your upline, your company, or your products or comp plan. It's based on you. In this book, we will assume you have joined a company, and are satisfied it's a good company.

I read a lot of MLM training books and find most of them fluff and padding. I hate fluff. A good part of a fluff MLM book is a chapter on 'what to look for in a good networking company'; you won't find that in this book. I assume if you are reading this book, you are already IN a company, and I'll save the fluff for my belly button.

If you are very green, perhaps you do need that beginner's book, but this book is not about picking the right company. This book teaches how you can brand yourself as either a product-based or opportunity-based expert that will make you attractive to prospects, using the EASIEST Internet or technological tools available so you can close sales and sign up recruits, and hit the big pay.

You will find a lot of ideas here. You do not have to use all of them, nor do you need to do them all at once. That is not the plan. I want you to have a good idea of what to do, and what different methods and tools are out there are so you can pick from them depending on the amount of time you have for this process. Some are faster and easier to implement than others.

The bottom line is this, if you are determined to be a $10,000 per month earner (as a minimum), you will have no choice but to follow what is in this book. If you do, I can tell you that you will find 100 times the success than the networker who is just buying leads and hoping people will watch the company video and join up.

Using the plans in this book, you can make most of your recruiting seem like it's going on autopilot. Now, you will still need to reach out and speak to prospects. But, because of how you frame yourself, as an expert, you will find that by the time a prospect speaks with you, they are pre-sold, and ready to join. So view the work you do now, setting up yourself as an 'authority,' as an investment and if you have to put some recruiting on hold for a few hours a day while you set this process up, so be it. This is the way it is today. It won't take long.

Portability Advantage

Keep this in mind; while no one wants to consider this, you may not always be with the networking company you are presently in. By branding yourself, and not your company, you are free to move to a new opportunity.

Let me share two funny stories to illustrate what I mean. While I was at the top level with a big MLM company, one of my midlevel distributors, who I liked personally, leased a new car and ordered vanity plates (or tags). His new license plates now had the initials of our company and the letters OKAY. Years later, I found him doing sales on eBay, and connected with him. When we met up, he was driving an old rusted car, with the same plates more than 15 years later. I was no longer with that company, and was working corporately with a different MLM. When I saw him driving with those same plates, it reminded me once again to not brand the company, but yourself.

By contrast, another leader in that same old company had come over from Herbalife. He had been very successful there, and was just as successful in our company too. He drove a very luxurious car, with the vanity plate, 'AskHow' on it. I learned he had that same plate during his Herbalife days. Lesson here is this: brand yourself (Askhow works for any company, by getting people to ask you how you can afford such a nice ride), whereas branding your company only promotes the company, and at worse can look embarrassing if you are not successful.

Branding yourself is portable.

One more story of my downline. There was one fellow in Europe, who, behind my back and against my advice and the policies and procedures of the company, had his car professionally painted with our company name and logo, etc. on it in BIG A$$ letters the size of a cow. His car was covered with the name of the company and its key product, urging people to use the product. This is the sort of thing that works for Coke, since everyone knows what Coke is. But when you are in a networking company, many of us do not want prospects to know the name of the company until they are in a meeting.

It got so bad that we had to have him NOT bring the car to opportunity meetings, because some prospects thought they would have to paint their car too. People would just turn around and drive off. Still others thought that he must be making big money because of his car, and wanted to do the same thing. It became a disaster. Just as an aside, he came from a rich family, who paid about $6,000 for this paint job.

I'm sure they paid just as much to remove it all.

By painting the name of the company on his car, his prospects knew what he was up to before he got into their driveway.

He lost control of the information flow.

Now, you might think, 'We don't do meetings in our company, so how does that apply to me?'

I'll tell you how.

Usernames.

I've seen newbies get Skype accounts with their company's name as part of their username.

Eg. 'AmwayHeroinGreenBay'

Subtle.

It's just like painting your car.

You are going to learn how to control the information flow and that will put YOU into the driver's seat.

Let's do it.

So, first lesson, brand yourself, and not your company.

The New Rules of Engagement for Network Marketing Success

The common denominator among all MLM or Network Marketing companies is person to person marketing. It can be 'warm market' or cold market, but it is person to person. But let's face it; person to person marketing can mean something very different in this era of social media. There are major differences from the time when MLM really began back in the early 1950s. The Internet has changed how we do 'person to person' marketing.

And it's vital to know the rules of engagement to win in this era.

The 'BUSY' Challenge

People have 'less time' today, and therefore it appears that they have a shorter attention span. It's really important to note here the difference:

People don't actually have shorter attention spans (people have not changed) – but today there are more competing messages vying for our attention – (times have changed) – so we may have to make our point in less time.

Network Marketing Savvy

Most people, if not all, are aware of network marketing and working at home. The fact that nearly everyone has heard about networking is a plus because they don't believe it's illegal or a pyramid scheme. Not only that, everyone knows that some people work at home, and that a 'home-based business' is very normal. Networking and affiliate marketing is not that strange a concept. Even people without a business at home have a home-office!

Today, people ARE open to having a business, especially home based. They know they can't rely on their jobs, the government, the economy, or the social safety net. In this economy, many are seeking additional income and don't need to be persuaded that they should be earning more. No one believes in the 40-40-40 plan anymore, and young people have never heard of it (work 40 years for $40,000 per year and retire with a $40 golden watch).

Change and Technology for better lead capture....

Capturing a lead just means getting someone into your sales funnel (or 'process').

Network Marketing originated in meeting rooms and hotels. Your grandfathers' MLM was the province of grand orators, "speechifiers," as Jed Clampett might say. Those who did well had a way with words and the ability to get someone to a meeting.

Those who were 'awkward' with words were not as lucky as those who were comfortable in making a presentation either one-on-one or to a group.

Times change, but people don't.

Good communication is just as essential as it was in 1950 or in 1776.

But the good news is that technology is making it easier and easier for those who are not natural born communicators to prospect and build their business.

Today more than ever, we can leverage technology to speak for us.

It's easier today.

This all started a few years ago....remember the days when you popped a 'tape' into a player to listen to music?

In the 1970s, technology entered the world of MLM. Cassette recorders and players were more and more common and in the early 1980s, VHS tapes could be copied cheaply, so great speakers could be recorded and duplicated via VHS tapes, allowing networkers to take 'the meeting' to prospects, rather than try and force the prospect to the meeting room.

Entire companies and distributorships were built on the use of tapes to 'get' folks interested and 'pre-sold' before attending a live event. This was a major change, but you still had to get that prospect to watch the tape.

How Ronald Reagan changed Networking...

Something else happened in the 1980s. With the wave of conservative politics in the US, deregulation in long distance telephone companies took place. What did this mean? Low cost long distance calling meant two things to networkers; one, that distributors could start building over long distances using the phone, and two, and most importantly, was the rise of the 'conference call.'

A few generations ago, the idea of a pager, a 'beeper' as they were known, were for the sole use of 'important' people. If you heard a pager beep, it was usually in an expensive restaurant where a surgeon was being called away to perform an emergency operation.

Just like 'beepers,' a conference call was something that only heads of state or heads of corporations attended. That was until deregulation, when network marketers discovered that it was easier to get a prospect on to a conference call than in a meeting room. One of the early pioneers of conference calls was Herbalife's Larry Thompson. I had the privilege of listening to a very small meeting with Thompson and 12 key networkers discuss how this whole conference call system started.

It turned out that a media company had purchased a large block of telephone time and was going out of business. The block of conference call time was picked up by Thompson, who had just quit his post as the Vice President of Herbalife to become a Herbalife distributor, to in-effect 'prove that anyone could build a successful Herbalife distributorship' during a time when a lot of their leaders were quitting.

As luck (or opportunity) would have it, Thompson found this conference call company and used it to deliver his message over the phone. He said he named his idea the 'Satellite Conference Call System' because it sounded very modern and exciting. It was all marketing.

Long story short, these calls rebuilt Herbalife back into a major force, and made a fortune for Thompson. Sadly, it ended badly for Larry, as Mark Hughes, founder of Herbalife, jealously kicked Thompson out of Herbalife, concerned he was getting 'too powerful' within the company.

Thompson is an MLM guru, a legend, and a great teacher. From that beginning, conference calling was born.

As more and more telephone companies began competing for long distance, conference calling and 'almost free' long distance calls became commonplace, and nearly every MLM company or team provided conference calls.

However, as time went on, attending a 'conference call' no longer had the pizzazz that it once did. Once very expensive to set up, conference calls are now free. It is now 'just as hard' or 'just as easy' to get some-one on a conference call as it was to a 'Business Opportunity Meeting' in a hotel in the old days.

And once again, more change...

As soon as everyone got used to 'conference calling,' there was a method to do a live group 'meeting'....

The Webinar.

Webinars had been around for a while, became less and less expensive, and more and more people got connected to the net.

Today, they can now be attended by people through their smartphones, tablets, or plain vanilla computers.

The Rise of Electronic Gatekeeper – and how to SMASH through it!

Now, the deregulation of the long distance companies made Telco's compete on local services too. Almost overnight, everyone got voicemail on their phone.

In the past, people actually answered their phone, because they could not see who was calling before picking up the 'receiver.' Back in those days, if you called a prospect, you would get through.

Once voicemail and caller ID became common and cheap, people could pick and choose who they spoke to.

The challenge created by this change is straightforward.

Think of it this way: if you want to reach a 'big shot' prospect, you must to go through their 'gatekeeper,' usually an assistant. Gatekeepers are employed to prevent you from reaching these 'important people.'

But today, technology is the poor man's gatekeeper.

What does this mean for you?

Try to call someone today who doesn't know you.

For example, a prospect opts-in to your capture page, and leaves a telephone number to get an "ethical bribe."

Call them, and their smartphone alerts them to the fact that someone they don't know is calling from some area code they don't recognize, and they guess it's some spammy telemarketer, often forgetting they opted-in for more info on your program. Perhaps they are just not interested in talking at the moment. Most people don't leave 'home' (landline) numbers on your opt-in form, and many don't even have them anymore. It's not easy to reach someone with a gatekeeping smartphone.

Now try to email that person. Once again, their email program shows them a portion of your email, so unless you can write a dynamite email, your message is ignored.

> FYI: If you can't write a 'dynamite email,' I have 3 books full of them. Just copy and add them into your email account and you'll find your phone ringing – see the end of this book to learn how to get them.

Not only that, often the email program moves your message into the 'promotions' section – if it's a Gmail account – or may even consider your message spam.

Once again, you have to deal with the electronic gatekeeper.

Marketing is not easy. Even if someone does opt-in to your list, you are forced to 'push' your message, until they either look at it, or unsubscribe from your list.

PUSH, PULL, and Attraction Marketing Explained

This book is all about EASY ways to beat the electronic gatekeeper. I'll show you how solve this challenge so that you have the best chance of a) pushing past the gatekeeper, and or b) attract prospects using 'pull' marketing rather than 'push' marketing.

You can call pull marketing 'Attraction Marketing' – you are pulling or attracting your prospect.

Once you understand the science of marketing, you can produce the results you desire. Attraction Marketing works only if we create enough reasons to create attraction. That is what you will learn how to do.

It's 90% of the reason why people are successful in networking. In the old days, 'Attraction Marketing' meant a good suit/dress, being a great speaker, having a nice car, great people skills, etc. Today, because of the Internet and the methods/tools you'll learn here, you don't need those things, because you are not 'belly to belly' as much as those heroes of the past. Today, you need different tools to achieve MLM success.

No matter how difficult you THINK networking is, it is a lot easier and less expensive today. Today, the Internet and technology have leveled the playing field if you follow this new system.

So, if you can read and take action, you are ready to succeed!

It's all GOOD!!!!

NOTE:

While it may seem that I have left you with the impression that 'belly to belly' networking is a thing of the past, it's not. And for those who think belly to belly or live presentations are over, think again.

Consider major music recording artists. While there are perfectly recorded CDs and MP3 digital audios available to be purchased, people still pay hundreds of dollars to see (and barely hear) their favorite performers live.

The most powerful MLM conversions, epiphanies, upsells, and commitments happen at live events. Never, ever forget to promote live events to your team/prospects where possible.

That one statement could be the subject of a book, but for now, the point is this: with technology, I'll show you how to make YOU the brand, make YOU attractive, and even make YOU a guru...

But at the end of the day, it matters not what way you conduct your business, from coffee shops, hotel rooms, business centers, or at home on the phone and Internet because your prospect still has access to 'Google.'

And you are going to learn how to control the information they see.

What is your Brand?

I'm going to really get deep into the concept of Branding throughout this book – because so many of your downline will have a hard time when you try and teach this concept to them. Especially if they come from 'traditional' business backgrounds.

Nearly every 'traditional' marketing course teaches promoting your company brand, or company name. Branding is all important. How can your customers find you if you don't promote your company's brand?

Google or search the word 'branding' and you'll be taken to all sorts of pages about branding your company name or product name.

Perhaps some of you have come from an 'Internet Marketing' background where branding your product is just as important.

Early on in my network marketing journey, I would hear the mantra of 'branding' from those who came from 'corporate' backgrounds.

"Why doesn't the company promote its name more, we need to have 'name-recognition!'?"

But traditional marketing and network marketing are not the same thing.

In MLM or networking, the concepts of Branding are the opposite of both traditional and Internet Marketing.

There are two things you must learn:

1) If you are in Amway, that is NOT your brand, that's Amway's brand.

2) You don't want 'name-recognition.'

Get this straight:

YOU are your brand.

AND YOU DON'T WANT NAME-RECOGNITION of your COMPANY NAME!

I want to make this Very Clear – your brand is NOT your company – it's **YOU**.

Now, your MLM company may not mind you promoting their brand, because for them it's just good to have brand awareness. However, for YOU, as a distributor – you are YOUR own company, you are an Independent Distributor, and therefore your brand is YOU.

For some people this is going to be the most important lesson from this book.

Let me explain...

Imagine Amway, one of the most well-known networking companies in the world. If you were promoting Amway, and your prospects knew that, few would respond to your message. Not because Amway is a bad company, but because your prospects THINK they know all about that opportunity. Now, truthfully, few people outside of Amway really know Amway's compensation plan, or that they market more than soap. However, that's not important. What is important is what's in the head of your prospect. They THINK they know enough about Amway to NOT venture further down that sales funnel.

If your prospect believes they know all about your company, your chance of getting them to move forward falls by 99%. You have to battle all these preconceptions in their mind.

Now add in the 'Google' factor.

Very quickly, any company can become known on the net. The more exposure there is, the more likely your prospect will have heard of your company. If you brand your advertising and lead generation with your company name or their lead product in such a way that it is easy for a prospect to figure out what company you are representing prior to them contacting you, or opting-in to your lead campaign email system, they are less likely to do so.

The ability to search on the Internet quickly is a double-edged sword. There are good and bad sides to it. I was coaching a very successful networker the other day on this very subject during one of my private consultation sessions. He was lamenting about some of his undisciplined downline who did not follow instructions. I asked him for an example. He said last week he helping a new person, and listened in on this newbie's calls to warm market.

He said, "I was listening in on a call my new guy was making to a friend of his – they had been in another company together previously. My guy had the script that I had given him, including what to say if interrupted. Could he stick to the script? No. Here's what happened – in the middle of the script, his friend interrupted him with 'What's the name of the company?' My new guy just froze on the phone, paused, and then said 'XYZ Co.... have you heard of it?' The prospect said no, but right away, you could hear the prospect typing on his keyboard at home, bringing up everything Google had on the company name. Now, as you know, so many competitors will bait Google with negative sites with each company's keywords and name in order to get leads. So, you know what happened, my guy is going on with his pitch, while his prospect is at home just half-listening, clicking away and reading all the crap that competitors spam the net with to lure away our prospects. We lost his attention, and when it came to invite him to our webinar, he said. 'Oh, I'll just watch one of these YouTube videos, and get back to you.'"

Now, this story not only shows the need to follow a script in the day and age of the search engine, but more importantly, it shows what your prospect is going to do as soon as they know any word that is searchable. Even on a mobile phone, people will search out anything you tell them.

Bottom line: YOU must learn to control the flow of information, which is the secret sauce that I'll be revealing soon.

How To Prospect like an Upline

The Process

No doubt you have a process to follow when showing a prospect your opportunity. It will be something like this:

1) Short opportunity video

2) Webinar/conference call/live meeting

3) Closing call or three-way call or team call

4) Further exposure if needed – a training, event, etc.

> *FYI: In my Mindset book, I outline this process much more, and really hammer it home. You can read more about the Mindset book and how it can set you up for success – for more details see the end of this book.*

Now your process is likely much more elaborate and contains more steps. The fact is, better minds than ours know the process that is best for your company, so in general, at first you should follow the tried and true method as you gain more experience; you can adapt it later.

But the point I want to make now is this: recruiting is a process, not an event. You need to realize it is the same for the lead capture process. Collecting leads is a process, not an event. It's a much shorter process, but you are still 'recruiting' a person – to become your 'prospect'.

What is vital is Branding.

What is the difference between you and your successful upline?

Why is it your successful upline can take people through the process and you feel you can't? The process is the same, the products are the same, it's all the same, except for one thing: you.

Why? Because, whether they know it or not, your upline styles themselves as an expert. Either consciously or unconsciously, they come across with authority and communicate from a position of strength.

This is what you are going to learn and do.

When you are the expert, your entire posture over the phone will change. Why? Because when you know that your prospect is predisposed to believe and respect you – your phone delivery changes. Your prospect feels good about you, and feels privileged to follow you through the process. They might say 'no,' but it's a real no, a no after the process ends. But the more people you take entirely THROUGH the process, the more yes's you will have.

Your closing rate will soar.

Not only that, those 'no's' will stay in your autoresponder system longer now, and you'll be surprised that a few months later, they will turn into 'yes's'.

By being an 'expert' or authority, you will find building your business a charm, not a chore.

When you follow what is outlined in this book, you will find people answer your phone calls, they call your conference call on time, attend your webinars, and follow up on your emails. Why? Because in their eyes, you are a 'someone.'

As much as I don't like the practice of buying leads, and find these leads the worst, this Branding method will give you the edge you need to wring out the best from this source.

The fact that you can demonstrate to your prospect that you are an authority and are known on the Internet as a success will be the big difference in your business. If you can find success with purchased leads, you will find 100 times more success with leads you generate yourself after following these Branding steps.

So, we are not going to change the process; we are going to change how your prospect views you before, during, and after you take them through the process.

Where is the best place to bury a dead body?

Lemonade anyone?

In my opinion, there is only one way to work with a negative that you can't change and that is to embrace it and turn it into a positive. Turn lemons into lemonade.

There is a way to make Google and the Internet work for you.

You'll learn how to step by step, but here's the idea:

Instead of hiding the name of your company, we will give your prospect something to search for. We will now factor their desire to search into our recruiting by branding you – and in turn make some lemonade.

So, when the time is right, you tell your prospect to search these key-words, "Mary, go to Google, type in 'Your-name, your-expertise' tell me what you see."

For example "Jane Smith Nutrition Expert"

Because we are going to set you up right, this search will produce enough links about YOU to fill page 1, or more on Google.

Okay Colombo fans:

"Where's the best place to hide a dead body?"

Give up?

"On page 2 of Google."

You only need to have 10 or so links to take the coveted first page of Google, and you can because Google is NOT searching for your company name, but for YOUR name, and your expertise can easily fill up the first page.

Take a second and re-read the paragraph above.

This is the key. You are controlling the search request, and thus the flow of information. You control it by telling your prospect what to search for, and the order to search for it. You will learn this is a lot easier to do than you think right now.

We are going to refer to this set of search terms, Your Name and Your Expertise, as the 'Secret Sauce Keyword Formula' from here on in.

You can tell them to do this when you speak to them, you can make it a tagline on your business card, you can add it to your email signature, but mostly you will tell them to do this in your first 'conversation.' That could be on the phone, or in an email, or even face to face in circumstances where it makes sense.

What will they see?

They will see page one of Google filled with links back to you as an expert, videos, images, blogs, and social media pages.

'Wow' is what they're thinking.

Now you're wondering, do I have the skills to make this work?

I'll teach you what to do. And if you have email and searching skills, you have enough experience to follow the instructions in this book to control the Internet, rather than allow it to take away your power. You will also have a powerful skill to teach your team too.

Don't worry about the how; it's not hard, and you'll learn what to do.

Or you can outsource the work.

But whichever way you choose to set up your branding, you are going to know what your prospect is going to see. You will also learn how to command Google to bring up what YOU want when someone types in "Your name and a keyword for your expertise." For example, if you are in a wellness program, and you sell a DNA profile, you could create pages that will pop up with your name and the acronym 'DNA.' You'll learn how to set your material to cause your prospect to search you out ON YOUR TERMS.

Jane Smith DNA Anti-Aging Expert

Now, this is not a book on SEO (or Search Engine Optimization), but you'll learn enough about searching to make this system work.

What you'll learn by the end of this book is: what to do and what to say to appear like an expert authority to Google… and any prospect who 'Googles' your name.

How to Position YOURSELF as an Expert or an Authority

In the past when I taught this training during expensive weekend semi-nars, a few people would come up on breaks and ask, 'how can I be an authority or an expert when I'm not?'

Let's address that question.

In the days before the Internet, the definition of an expert was someone who either came from afar, had an accent, or carried a brief case. In other words, someone you did not know, or was 'different from you,' and therefore seemed like they knew more than you.

In the very narrow terms we are covering here, it is the only difference between you and your prospect. As long as you have joined your net-working program prior to your prospect, in all likelihood you know more about the company, the products, the 'sales funnel,' or process than they do. It's that simple – in that sense you are an expert.

You hold the facts, they want the facts.

Therefore, you as the 'fact holder' are an expert, or an authority on this subject. Not only that, but adding into the mix that you have the infor-mation contained in this book, which you can teach to your team and later to your prospect – makes you an expert.

You hold all the cards.

Of course, in the fullness of time, you will keep learning and learning and you will be much more knowledgeable than at present, so don't sweat it.

What if my prospect is a 'big-shot' MLM type?

Well, that person will sure respect you and listen to you once they see page 1 of the Google search full of your info. They may know more about MLM than you do, but they will see you as a product expert. And they will respect that.

What are experts today anyway?

In the world of the Internet, anyone who puts up a website and some supporting information appears as an expert if they follow a few steps that we will cover here. You will have to embrace this idea – that you must become an authority in the eyes of your prospect in order to compete on the net or you will lose the game of Network Marketing in the days of the Internet. Decide right now if you are going to be a professional in this business or just a hobbyist.

But don't forget hobbies cost money; they don't earn you profits. You owe it to yourself, your family, and anyone you have sponsored to be professional. This is not about time commitment, it's about treating your MLM business like the BUSINESS it is.

What about saturation? But how many Experts can there be?

It's funny that we ourselves ask this question, when prior to the Internet, prospects asked us the silly 'saturation' question.

Let me cover this answer in a couple of ways. First, because MOST people will NOT do what I am showing you here, no matter how many people read this book, there will never be too many 'experts.' This book contains training that I have taught to networkers who paid over $10,000 for 3 days at fancy resorts. Folks who paid big money and still went home and didn't 'get around to it.'

Taking action is what leaders do. Money is often wasted on some folks.

Now, I have reversed the cost, found easier ways, and faster methods, and sell this book for only $20 or so. But still, you will find many more people who will buy this book, but do nothing. It's the same with MLM. How many people take action?

I know that's not you; if you are on my newsletter list I know it's not you.

Really.

(go to www.davidwilliamsMLMauthor.com to get on it!)

Secondly, because we are using your keywords PLUS your name, the search becomes unique.

By the end of putting this simple plan in effect, you will have learned how to show up as an expert on the net, and succeed at your prospecting. You will be able to apply the secret sauce keyword formula on a shoe string budget, or, if you have funds, you can have it all outsourced to save you time.

There is no reason for you to not set yourself up as an expert and succeed. All that matters is if you do it or not.

Be the person who does it.

I'm still not sure: Do I have to learn everything there is to know about my company or networking before I declare myself as an authority or expert?

Brian Tracy and I were talking back stage many years ago. He remarked that a person could read 20 books on one subject to master it. I'm sure that is true for most things today too. But you don't have to read that many books for our purposes.

Here is a story to illustrate my point: Two men were camping and sleeping in their tent. In the middle of the night, they hear loud growls and the shredding of their campsite. One of the men peeks outside through the flap, and sees a 12-foot grizzly bear raging through their empty food containers, and they realize it's only a matter of moments before the bear smells them in the tent.

They decide to make a run for it, and one pauses to put on his running shoes. The other says, "Why are you wasting time putting on those shoes, come on, you'll never outrun a grizzly bear!"

His companion keeps putting on his shoes, and says, "That's true, but I don't have to outrun the bear; I just have to outrun you."

It's the same here – you only need to know more information than your prospect. You don't need to know everything about your business, just more than your prospect.

And you know what?

By the time you have set this system up, you will have learned a lot. A month later, you will have learned a lot more and in a few months you really will feel like an authority as you build your team and prosper in your program. It will happen pretty quickly.

So, don't worry about bears or prospects. Let's roll up our sleeves and put things in motion to make YOU the expect authority that will allow you to bring in prospect after prospect and build your team.

What kind of Authority or Expert?

When setting yourself up as an authority or expert, you have two good options. Just as you can lead with the product in MLM or lead with the opportunity, you will need to decide what you will become an authority or expert on before you create your Internet presence (of course you can do both, but it can be confusing, so I would pick one type first, and apply the secret sauce keyword formula, and after do the same thing for your other type of expertise – don't think of it as twice the work – but rather 'twice the income').

For example, if you are in an environmental company (perhaps air filters), or a wellness company (anti-aging, weight loss, vitamins, etc.), or a deeper niche of one of these, you can chose to be an expert in the product expertise side. Weight loss, fitness, nutrition, etc., there are many options.

An example could be Jane Smith Anti-Aging (and/or adding your company name. I like to NOT add the company name, BUT you can, it's just a preference). Just note that Google will fill in words after the search term you type in as suggestions based on what people search for. For example, if you type into Google:

mary had

you will see

mary had a little lamb

etc.

The reason I don't want to have a company name there is so, once again, I can control the flow of information. However, if you are dealing with people that have already seen the majority of your process and you are 'closing them' on why they should sign up with you, it could be argued that you want to be seen as an expert among those associated with your company.

Now, you could instead chose opportunity, i.e.:

David Williams residual income specialist

Or Jane Smith deregulation income specialist, etc., etc.

You just need to make a choice since you are the person who will be telling these search terms to your prospect. Decide what you are most comfortable with.

There are pros and cons to choosing product over opportunity, and we will cover these before you make your decision. Most of you will have already decided, based on your interest.

Product Niche Authority or Expert

If you read my book How to Recruit Doctors into your Wellness MLM, you have seen a system built around the psychology of this entire concept, that the Doctor is already the 'authority' by virtual fact that they are 'Doctors' with regard to health.

As you know, doctors can earn millions in MLM. So there is no reason to not go down this road yourself. It does work. If you're not a doctor, you won't have that cachet that being a doctor has, but you can still become a wellness expert. I would suggest that in natural healing or natural health, 99% of the bloggers, commenters, authors, coaches, etc. are not formally trained, nor are they 'authorities' or 'experts' in any way different than what we are doing. Of course, most are dedicated to their niche and have spent a lot of time researching it, but not all. In any event, the only difference between them and you is time, and in our case we are not 'healers' – we are marketers.

You can position yourself on the net as an expert in your niche and as such, people are very likely to join with you, just as people like signing up with doctors. Now, it's good if you choose this area if you truly have a passion for your niche, so you can sound and show yourself as educated in the area.

I have met so many networkers who had an encyclopedic knowledge about their product and its health niche. If this is you – you are perfect for establishing yourself as an expert.

So if that's you, and you are reading this book, don't miss this opportunity to put all of your knowledge to use to help a large number of people, and to do yourself some good by building up a great big team. Just temper your natural inclination to use the 'fire-hose' approach (overkill) and ration-out your information. You will find it easy to follow this system and wonder why you never did it before.

The one drawback to focusing on wellness or a product niche is the portability factor. Look, no one wants to think about this, but companies come and companies go. If you spend a lot of time in a narrow niche, you limit what you can do with it if your company closes its doors or decides to go another direction. I realize that you are not going to even contemplate that happening, but it can.

So, if you are really 'into' your product niche, meaning you are going to go the extra mile (meaning extra time), to research and build up yourself as an expert, do so. It will serve you well. However, if you are more a 'business' minded type, stick to an opportunity niche.

Opportunity, Income Authority or Expert

Just as we mentioned above, if you choose income or opportunity as your 'expertise,' you have far more portability if you are forced (or decide) to change companies. As you are an expert on making money, or marketing, or lead generation, or something that leads to success in networking, you can fit any company. It is a much more portable choice.

The second advantage in choosing this area as your expertise is the fact that there are more people searching for a way to earn money than there are for very specific product niches. So you have more opportunity, (and more competition too) for finding leads. Now, because of the way we are going to show how to set yourself up, the fact that you have lots of competitors will not be an issue.

If I were NEW and starting now, with zero track record, I would go with my product niche. It will be easier, simpler and faster. However, if you know a great way to find leads, or you have some special teachable skill, that is useful for networkers, that is a great niche too.

Jane Smith Network Marketing Postcard Queen

Any decision is okay, just make a decision.

If you are really undecided, write me and tell me your feelings and reasons and I'll give you some feedback. DavidWilliamsAuthor@gmail.com

No matter which of the two sides you choose, the system you will use works equally well. Just pick the best one for you.

One more question I get after teaching this live is 'Oh, but is doing this duplicable?'

Heck yes! Now more than ever, with the tools and methods I will show you, you can make this system part of your getting started training for your team, giving them another reason to join with YOU.

Just point them into the direction of this book (which I thank you for), and once they have read it, and are ready, you'll be able to steer them in the right direction, which will set them up faster and thus earn you both money faster.

By the way, I'm not telling you to recommend this book just so I can make one more book sale; no, I am telling you to do this because you are leveraging your time by having ME train your team (via the book). If they tell you they won't invest in a book – 'can you teach me instead' – forget it; your time is more valuable.

Consider this: imagine if all of your team were listed on the net as experts when their prospects Googled them. Can you imagine how fast your team would grow?

You would do less explaining on follow up calls for them, on closing calls, and three-way calls too.

How much is that worth to you?

Think about how time you will save, and much you would earn in the process?

The "Professionals" MLM Gurus, etc...

Branding themselves as experts is what the pros do. The only difference is that they keep it to themselves, and don't teach it to their downline. I find that foolish at best, and offensive at worst. Show your team how to prosper, and you will prosper too.

So, what do my prospects want to know?

Before we get into how to set the secret sauce keyword formula up, I want to sum up our strategy.

Some of you who are a little Internet savvy have already picked it up, and won't even need to read the rest of this book. If that's not you, you're in good company – I had to learn this – but the good news is that it is easier now!

It took me a long time to realize that it was a loser's game to try and beat the Internet. Once I figured out the formula for 'lemonade,' I realized that it was just better to follow this method then to pretend people would not search online for things. It's part of our culture.

I do it all the time.

Think of it this way: right now, prior to setting yourself up as an expert or an authority, you are floating in the ocean as one of a million other drops of water, each one saying the same thing, with the same scripts, same autoresponders, same replicated websites, same marketing material, trying to sell your prospect to join with YOU.

If they ask you, 'why should I join with you?' you'll say 'It's not about me, it's about you, and by the way, we have access to my upline who is Mrs. Big Shot, who is able to break the rules of physics and spread herself so thin she will promise to help you build your business too.'

OR....

...you are someone who has wisely invested in this book. You have decided to take matters into your own hands, and create a situation where your prospect is already sold on working with you. They will not ask 'how are you doing in the businesses' because they will assume that you are successful based on what they have seen; they will not even ask about upline support, because they will be looking at YOU as their mentor. Even those with network experience will be impressed, and look forward to working with you.

You will sound strong on the phone, and speak from a position of authority and strength, because you know you appear strong. Your prospects are impressed, will take your calls, follow up with you, and, for those who say no or disappear, you know it's not because they found someone 'better,' it's just that they are not interested or serious about changing their lives.

You'll find rejection disappears and struggling ends. Your value to your downline, your company, and to your prospects increases. And, as an expert, there is no more hard selling, closing becomes easy, and you become irresistibly attractive.

What Do Prospects want MOST when seeking an opportunity?

When I started writing this chapter, I remembered a page from a book by Michael Dlouhy, a very clever networker. His book, Success In 10 Steps! is available on the web. He has a very 'in your face' style, but it's full of good MLM common sense and is perfect for any network newbie OR anyone who has not found success. Google it and read it.

For now, I just want to relate some research that supports the importance of you in the recruitment process.

Dlouhy conducted a questionnaire of a cross section of new recruits in network marketing companies. He offered each subject 10 items that could potentially trigger someone to join, and he asked them to arrange them in importance to their decision to sign up. These were the factors, in order of importance to the new distributor:

- Company literature on display
- Compensation plan/potential income

- Was there training
- Person that presented the opportunity
- Products
- Corporate management experience
- Upline support ability
- Corporate image
- Distributor kit provided
- Getting in first in a particular region

Before I give you the list in order as the fresh recruits arranged it, perhaps you would like to write down your ranking of the list. In other words, how do you rate these in order of importance for someone joining you and your company?

Okay, now that you have written your list, turn the page and see the results of the survey.

1) Person that presented the opportunity

2) Upline support ability

3) Was there training

4) Compensation plan/potential income

5) Products

6) Getting in first in a particular region

7) Company literature on display

8) Corporate image

9) Distributor kit provided

10) Corporate management experience

*Based on a survey in Success In 10 Steps! by Michael Dlouhy.

So you see the lesson from this survey of new distributors. This is how you must think; you need to think like your prospect. Now, this survey was taken in pre-Internet days, so don't think in terms of 'presentations,' but in terms of who is bringing the prospect to the table, in other words, who the sponsor is. Most of it comes down to you. You are the upline support; you are either the trainer or you can demonstrate that there is training. You must be able to show the compensation plan well enough for prospects to see the income in it.

People want to know you can show them the way. They don't expect 'personal' handholding. It's no longer practical.

This is the reason why we NEED to make you an expert. Experts don't know everything, but they know where everything is.

Lucky for you, it's much easier to show up as an expert thanks to the Internet today than in the past!

How to become a Page 1 Star! – How to make Google your friend

The Secret Sauce...

There are two ways to be visible on Google – the long way or the easy way.

The long way involves endless SEO (Search Engine Optimization) efforts with the objective to link keywords to your website. We are not going here.

Your aim is to brand YOU, not to create a website with lots of hits (if that is what you want, you do need to learn all about SEO or hire some high-priced specialists to do it for you).

Our real aim is to get YOU looking like an 'authority' or expert.

So, here is the Secret Sauce.

The secret sauce is all about creating a small addition that you add in to your normal phone script to prospect.

For example

"Hey Mr. Prospect, if you want to see how qualified I am to be your upline/coach/nutritional teacher/etc. just go to Google, type in my name 'John Doe Nutritional coach' (or 'Jane Smith MLM guru' or 'Juice Plus Expert' or 'Organo Gold Coffee Professional' or 'Zija Leader') and tell me what you see?"

Or add it to your email signature – in addition to any invitation to look at your videos, etc., add your chosen keywords, for example add this line – "Go ahead, check me out – Google: 'Jane Smith Nutrition Expert'."

What will your prospect see?

They will see all of the first page of their Google search come up with search links about you.

You can do this as you are talking on the phone. Let them click away, and after a few seconds, say "Mr. Prospect, you can read all about me later, but the real point is…" and bring the conversation back to your business.

You can also add the secret sauce keyword formula to emails as well, inviting your prospect to 'check you out' by telling them what to search for!

After your prospects clicks on some of your links (often they just have to see that the entire first page of Google is filled about you), they will be convinced about your 'authority'.

In the MLM world, they will now be quite happy to have you for their upline.

Why? It is because you gave them a reason to do so when they searched for you on Google.

How do you do this?

By creating just a few web pages – for example one video on YouTube is a page – and each page contains your name and your chosen keywords.

I'll share with you how easy this is and how you'll do it, but first let's talk about your keywords, or the words you are going to tell your prospect to search for. Because these will be the words we use to add to you videos, webpages, and social media sites, etc.

Remember: Once you complete the secret sauce keyword formula, you must update your prospecting script.

For example, when you are speaking to your prospects, be sure you tell them to "Check me out on the web, can you go to Google? Okay, type this in, 'Jane Smith Nutrition Expert' and tell me what you see?" (Caps are not required) By asking them 'what do you see,' you confirm they spelt your name right, and second, you are getting them to 'do things' – this book is not about psychology, but there is an edge you gain through a process called 'compliance' – getting people to do what you tell them – your prospects quickly get use to the idea of you leading them.

Finding the right keywords and content

Now that you understand how the secret sauce works by establishing your credibility on search engines, it is time to choose the right keywords.

Your keywords will depend on the niche you wish to be an expert in. This can be a product or opportunity. So where do you find the right keywords and the right content?

You need not worry about SEO or SEO keywords. However, you need to establish how you wish to portray yourself to others. Imagine this – you are on a Skype call with someone who is not known to you. Now, if you tell them to search for 'Jane Smith Nutrition Expert' and if you're positioned on the first page of Google in the form of various links, imagine the impact on your prospect!

This positions you as a leader in the industry. No one cares about digging deeper beyond page one.

So the million-dollar question is how do you decide on these keywords? You have to correlate your product or opportunity to what goes in the industry.

An important point to understand here is that SEO efforts here will not matter much, because your prospect has been told what to search for. So the point is to position yourself as an expert when people search for you in any form possible.

It's at this point you need to decide if you are 'Jane Smith Juice Plus Expert' or 'Jane Smith Deregulation Expert, or Anti-Aging Expert, Body-building and Nutrition Coach, DNA Expert, etc.'

Now that we have keywords and content, we are going to do a few things on the net to make ourselves known.

We will cover areas in the practical side of this book for each search result, but here is a basic checklist for you:

- LinkedIn page
- FB page IF YOU HAVE IT already
- 10 plus YouTube videos
- Pinterest account
- Images – various sites
- Google Plus account
- Google Blog
- Twitter
- BrandYourself.com
- Amazon Profile Page

Extra if you want:

- SlideShare
- AboutMe.com
- Wordpress or other sites/blogs

We will cover each of these in the chapter called 'Social Media Short Cut' unless they have their own chapter, like LinkedIn and YouTube.

One last thing:

While most of this book will deal with branding your business via the Internet, there are still some areas that are offline and need to be addressed.

Business cards. Most companies have stock business cards that you can order or have printed with their name and logo. Usually, as long as you put the words 'Independent Distributor' on the card, you can use their name and logo.

But for what? In this day and age, most savvy people know what the words 'Independent Distributor' mean.

They mean 'unceasing phone calls' or harassment.

These cards are only useful for you when you attend your own company sponsored events or rallies. Trade them with other Independent Distributors to build up your three-way call buddy list, but don't use them for recruiting.

Don't give away your strength. Allowing your prospect to know the name of your company, by reading your business card (or your email signature, e.g. Harold Punter, Independent Direct Distributor, Amway – Come and learn about the World of Amway – Much more than soap!) will drive people away from you.

And FYI: I'm not picking on Amway here, I have the utmost respect for it. I could use any company name. The more well-known your company name is, the harder it is to build your business if you don't brand yourself.

But that does not mean that building a 'brand new' company is easer – in the days of the Internet, a 'hot new company' name goes viral quickly and once again you are back to square one.

You need to control the flow of Information in the Information age.

We are in a knowledge-based economy now, and therefore you need to understand that YOU have the knowledge NEEDED by your prospect.

You know how they can solve their financial problems.

But in order for them to learn how to solve their problems through your company, you need to feed them specific knowledge in a specific order.

Changing the order or the amount of this knowledge will at best mean success or failure – so YOU need to stay in control.

If you need business cards, you can design your own. Turn your card into an ad leading to your voicemail message, as well as your contact information.

What do you put on your card?

Always think WIIFM – What's in it for me?

What keeps your prospect up at night?

No one cares to 'hear about an exciting new company call 555...' you must craft a compelling message to get someone to call. However, this book is about branding, and not copywriting (that's in the next book!).

So let's see some clever business cards.

Remember, your business card has only one purpose:

To get someone to call you.

How to immunize your prospect from 'sponsor shopping'

'Sponsor shopping'

What is sponsor shopping?

Well, let's say a prospect somehow falls into your lead system. Through you he learns the name of your company, and decides it's a company he wants to join.

Once he knows the company name, he can Google it and see what other distributors are out there and what they may offer him to join with them instead of you.

This is not a nice thing to happen, not at all. Often, you may not even know that it took place.

However, in the age of the Internet, it's more likely to happen than not.

But by following what you have learned here to show up as an expert, you can really nip this in the bud.

Because you know your lead system and your sales funnel, you know when your prospect learns the name of your company, i.e. perhaps you told him, emailed him, or you sent him a video that shared this info with him.

As soon as that has happened, you can 'immunize' your prospect from sponsor shopping by using an email much like this:

(put in subject line here that makes sense)

Hi Bob,

Great talking to you about Juice Plus.

Juice Plus has changed my life, as well so many others. You're in good hands working with me because I'm an expert on it.

But hey, don't take my word for it; just type this into Google and see for yourself:

Jane Smith Juice Plus Expert

Once you have seen for yourself that I know what I'm talking about, get back to me. I can teach you how to set up a great team for marketing Juice Plus, where to find leads, and I'll show you how to get into profit fast.

<Put in short testimony about product>

Call me; I'm here, and ready to work with you every step of the way.

Best,

Jane Smith

P.S. (put in a call to action, i.e. the next step in your sales funnel)

Doing this will stop sponsor shoppers in their tracks - as your prospect will now be confident in working with you; in fact, they will feel lucky to!

But David, what the heck do I say? The Short Secret of Content

Now it's only common sense that if you're going to grab all the places on page 1 of Google, you need to have a few (more than a few) different pages loaded with your secret sauce keywords.

But there is a catch... and the catch is called 'content.'

Content is the all the other 'stuff' on a page that supports your keywords.

For example, the page in this book you're reading now is about 250 words. If 5 of them were your keywords, think of the page as 'content' supporting your keywords.

So, as we learn about the places where you will be creating pages that show up as links on page 1 of Google (as per the secret sauce keyword formula), I'll answer the hardest question each of us has when it comes to creating a page, a post, a video, an image, blog, or a tweet…. or anything else you decide to create for the web.

"David, just what the heck do I say?"

This is the content. If you want to sound like you are 'in' with the 'Internet marketing' crowd, just say 'content is king' and smile knowingly.

And it is queen too.

Now this is why the Internet is so full of poor information. Because most content is just any old thing people paste into 99% of sites to get you to visit and get you to click on an advertisement to take your money.

This is what is called SEO, or search engine optimization, to get a site to show up high on the search engines with what looks like good information about whatever you searched for, gets you to click the link, and you see an ad that they think will appeal to you.

No doubt you have found that 99% of what you search for is just basic stuff you knew anyway. Go ahead, type in 'how to make money online' and what will you find?

Any in-depth answers to your question?

Or some come-on sales pages or blogs that are so basic that you wonder how someone could have even written them without feeling embarrassed.

Why? Because there is a link there for an ad, or a request for you to trade your email address for something that promises you an answer.

We have all been down that road before.

Content is so watered down (mostly) that I hardly use Google search for anything except specific items of interest (like, 'what sites will schedule Twitter posts' or 'how do I create channel art for my YouTube account').

Everyone is out there making sites to get leads by trying to make them bigger, better, and filling them full of keywords to get your email address, and then bombard you with their pitch.

So they are forced to keep their sites active (or Google will lower them in the search engine rankings) by constantly submitting weak, watered-down basic content that is worthless, OR by pulling out their hair creating truly valuable content. I can tell you, as someone who creates an email newsletter each week, this is not easy.

All the experts say you must follow this recipe to create a real presence online, so that you'll rank high in Google and people will find you and join your program or buy your stuff.

But if you follow this system, you're competing with everyone else – and you don't need to.

Why be 'one more'?

To get leads on the net yourself, for MLM, you would need to spend big bucks, and create an online machine.

BUT: Success comes from looking what everyone else is doing and doing the opposite.

Find leads other ways - and THEN show up as an expert when our prospect looks for us based on the secret sauce formula.

What is our task?

Create enough pages to show up on page 1 of a Google search based on our secret sauce keyword formula.

Now, we still need content, so I'm going to provide you with VERY creative, VERY simple, and UNKNOWN ways to get it that are PERFECT for our industry AND without you pulling out your hair either!

And let's face it; you don't need a lot, but I'm going to show you, in the following chapters, how to create a lot, just so you really see how easy it is, and how you can, especially for some social media sites, appear active without having to work hard at it.

I want you to be spending your time with prospects, not 'working on your site' or 'doing Facebook.'

I'll get into the nitty-gritty about each site in the following chapters, but I want to give you a good grounding here.

First, remember the success principle connected to our industry: Leverage.

In our quest to control Google, you can leverage a great deal of what you know, of what your company provides, and what is on the net already – without creating crappy content or investing a lot of time.

How?

Remember the motto of the Round Table '*Adopt, Adapt, and Improve*'?

By the way, 'Adopt, Adapt, and Improve' is how you need to approach every training you hear, every sentence uttered by your upline, every book you read, every audio you listen to, or every DVD you watch.

Internalize this concept.

When it comes to content – learn to re-purpose it.

> For example, I'll be showing you ways to get great product testimonials for YouTube on your products, so you'll have some great videos.

> From there, you can transcribe these testimonials.

> You now have 'text' content to use on a Facebook post.

> From that, you can edit 180 characters out of it, and put that into your Twitter feed.

> From the video, you can take a still image (easy), and add text to it and upload this image to Pinterest (Another happy customer of 'Juice Plus').

Now post that image on your blog, all with links back to you, tagged to you.

In this example alone, you have taken one medium (YouTube video), and turned it into 6 different pages that will show up when someone searched you by using the 'secret sauce keyword formula.'

Re-purpose.

Something as simple as a short testimonial.

It's worthwhile content. It's real.

It helps people. It's not worthless content.

Here's another example:

> You can read up on your product, and write yourself 200 words about it. Or hire someone to.

> Once you have it, re-purpose it into an audio by recording it yourself, or outsourcing it to Fiverr.com and paying $5 to have someone else record it for you.

> Put that audio on your free video editor as your sound track and create a simple video (you will see how simple this is later), and upload it to YouTube.

> Tweet about that video.

> Take a still image and upload that to Pinterest and to other image sites.

> Post that image on your blog.

And another example:

Call up a knowledgeable upline or sideline.

Record the call – there are free apps for this – or use a Skype recording add-on.

It's legal if you tell them – and you need to get their permission to use the interview anyway!

Do a SHORT interview with them about the product, or WHY the business works so well (pick a topic that a prospect wants to know about – WIIFM – what's in it for me).

Listen to the recording.

Type it up, or, if you want to, use rev.com to create a transcript for you – $1 per min – no minimum.

Edit the manuscript.

Turn it into a blog post, a Facebook post, and Tweet about it.

Take the best 30 seconds of the audio and turn it into a video.

From there, take out a still and it's an image.

Upload the video to your blog too, and upload the video to YouTube and the image to Pinterest.

You see?

By thinking of how you can adopt (use other people – leverage), adapt it for different social media sites, and improve (edit), you have re-purposed good quality content for many different platforms.

I'll be revealing more specific methods for each of the sites in the upcoming chapters to make this easy and efficient. In the end, you will have piles of content – more than you will ever need.

If you are efficient yourself, you can keep posting this content without it taking you very long each week, and you'll have such an abundance of material on the net leading back to you that your expert status will never be questioned.

LinkedIn - The Place for Grown-ups

www.linkedin.com

One place to gain professional clout and make your mark is LinkedIn.

If Facebook is high school, LinkedIn is university. LinkedIn can be a great tool for your brand, and if you like, for recruiting, because it's much more professional.

This book is only on the subject of branding, but if you do want to recruit on LinkedIn, you still need to set up the secret sauce formula to become an expert, especially if recruiting on a site like LinkedIn.

FYI: A good friend of mine uses LinkedIn to do all her recruiting (90% of it), and is in the $10K per month club.

TIP: Get Endorsed – You can find me on LinkedIn. I tend to connect with everyone – and I'm a serial endorser too – which means if you connect with me, you'll get 'endorsed' by me. You'll need my email address to prove you know me, so if you want to connect, please utilize davidwilliamsauthor@gmail.com.

Let's explore the profile...

To begin with, it's easy to create a profile and apply the secret sauce formula to your LinkedIn profile.

It's very simple to join. There's no need for me to walk your through it.

However, you need to set up your 'profile.' On LinkedIn, it's very much like an old-school resume or 'curriculum vitae.'

The rest of this chapter is a story about how I got humbled by a non-networker on LinkedIn:

Most people follow the LinkedIn example, as did I. I thought my profile was pretty good compared to the usual dull boring stuff found in the corporate world.

Most of the time, it's just networkers or related folks who connect with me. When we connect, I like to see what company my new connection is promoting.

A guy named Pete from Amarillo, Texas, asked to connect with me. I accepted and took a look at his profile to see what networking company he was with.

I read his profile and my jaw dropped open.

I was stunned.

I was astounded, humbled, and if I'm completely honest with you, I was a wee bit jealous.

His profile was the best I have ever read on LinkedIn. Period.

I'm going to provide you with his info so you can look him up – and feel free to connect with him, but resisted the urge to look until you read the rest of this section and my mini Q&A with him. You'll learn some sage advice from Pete.

There are two things we as networkers and communicators teach:

1) Always communicate in terms of WIIFM (What's In It For Me), i.e. from the prospect's point of view (a good question to know is 'what keeps my prospect up at night?')

and

2) Stories Sell, Facts Tell

This is basic 101 stuff – and yet when I read Pete's profile and realized mine was NOT following what I teach and preach – that's when I realized I had to go back to the basics! (FYI: I updated my profile in light of looking at Pete's, but I thought I would include the old one here just so you can see the difference.)

My Old LinkedIn profile:

David Williams has been a top earner and top performer in networking for over 25 years. He has worked all over the world building teams successfully. In the last five years, he has worked with corporations to develop MLM opportunities as well as top performers to create recruiting systems for their teams.

During that time, he also delivered 'insider only' high-priced seminars for 'the big dogs' on practical MLM: prospecting, recruiting, and team expansion.

In 2012, he decided to put into book-form some of the trainings he has done, and offer them online. Typically his work spreads word-of-mouth and word-of-mouse. Williams decided to present his insiders training at price levels that are affordable to anyone, but is not trying to disrupt the high-priced seminars business either. Rather, he feels that his readers are new and future leaders who are not even aware of these insider events, but will one day be seated there if they follow his systems.

Williams is not actively working any MLM program, but enjoys 8 different residual income sources and in multiple currencies.

His favorite MLM tips include:

- Fire your Upline
- Be the Upline you want
- Never stop recruiting

- How much money would you make today if my downline did what you did?

He hates 'fluff' training.

He writes an MLM email training letter that he sends weekly – you can sign up too at www.DavidWilliamsMLMAuthor.com

END OF OLD PROFILE

Now after I read Pete's LinkedIn page, I wrote him to say I was humbled by his profile.

Then I thought: I need to share his example and story with you.

So I asked him a few questions and permission to share his response.

David: "Pete, as the majority, the vast majority, of LinkedIn profiles are 'name, rank and serial number,' where did you get idea to use personal stories to share your past?"

Pete: "I believe the original idea came from Craig Wells (he's a LinkedIn expert), though the stories are mine."

David: "Did you write your profile yourself, or hire someone?"

Pete: "I wrote them myself. I actually hired someone to do my profile, but it was in the 'standard' format and ineffective; thus, I found Mr. Wells. I had taken a couple of copywriting courses, so I just put those lessons to work."

David: "Do you think anyone could sit down, look at their profile, and re-write it in the way you have – or do you think it's not possible for the average person?"

Pete: "It's definitely possible! I did. And trust me...I'm average :-)"

David: "Anything else you might want to add that would help out our readers?"

Pete: "I started working on my personal brand a few years ago. That's where most of my social media is centered around--PeteInc. My site is www.peteinc.com, my Twitter handle is @peteinc. I have a PeteInc Google page. The name of my LLC is Pete Inc Solutions.

"Not only is Pete my name, but it is an acronym for what I stand for as a leader: People Engaged Transform Each other.

"I have two hashtags that I try to use consistently with most brand messages: #WeAreMoreThanMe & #UnderYourLid (this is where every- thing starts...even the crazy stuff). These are actually books I intend to write as well, but I have to get my life in order first.

"Also associated with my 'brand' is my logo (still refining) and my 'tribe' (don't really have one yet, but am directing everything in this direction): The ALPHA Circle...Always Live Passionately, Honorably, Authentically.

"This is probably more than you were looking for, and I hope it helps. I've spent much thought on my personal brand because the one I had (and we ALL have one) was created 'unconsciously' and not aiding in what I was trying to accomplish...so I decided to do a brand 'makeover' and create a brand that more closely represented who I was and what I stand for.

"Anyone can do what I've done if they choose. The quality of the 'brand' will be determined by the quality of the questions they ask themselves and the level of honesty they use to answer those questions. It all starts #UnderYourLid :-)"

You can to go www.peteinc.com and click on Pete's LinkedIn button to access his profile if you are a LinkedIn member – if you are not, it's free to join.

Now if you have not skipped ahead, let me share with you what Pete does. He's is a top life insurance sales pro. Not a network marketer. He's a major earner. But nothing on his website would tell you that. No, his site is all about giving and his personal philosophy.

You can see that Pete is the real deal, not a 'slick sales guy' – quite the opposite – which has resulted in his success. It's attraction marketing at its best.

Study his words above.

You can do a 'makeover' on your profile too. Think about what you are trying to accomplish, and it will come. Keep referring back to Pete's as the example to emulate.

I'm glad Pete connected with me, and I'm super proud to share his profile with you!

Now if you are already on LinkedIn, take some action and do a makeover now. There is never a better time than today!

I did my makeover, and if you want to read it, just hop over to LinkedIn and see it for yourself.

If you want to connect with me, you'll need my email address: davidwilliamsauthor@gmail.com.

Channel YOU – YouTube can make you a STAR!

YouTube is your best friend when it comes to filling up page 1. As you know, Google searches for a variety of content, including YouTube videos, and positions the content on the first page because Google owns YouTube.

You will be creating a lot of videos – a minimum of 10, and there is no max.

Please, before you think this is a big chore, just read on. It's not as hard as you think, and I'll tell you what to say and how to do it. And if you want to succeed, you will do it.

Personally, I found making videos easy to do. I just figured it out by playing around with the software. Having said that, I now outsource my video making because of time commitments.

Added Benefit: There is always a chance that people find your videos without searching for you –but this is not our aim. It's just an unexpected benefit. And hey, it's not bad if there are a lot of videos online featuring you and positioning you as a leader or expert in the industry!

I'm not going to tell you a lot of 'how to set up a YouTube channel' because if you just Google that phrase, you'll find (at present count) over 256,000,000 websites and videos to explain it better.

If I did, that would be a lot of filler and padding for this book.

You would see right through that!

That said, I am going to provide you with the important aspects and tips that make this process faster and simpler to get your videos in line with the secret sauce keyword formula.

Of course, if you are someone who is comfortable sitting in front of your computer with the camera on, that is the easiest way to create videos, but if you don't want to be on camera, I'll explain how to do that as well.

Let's cover some basics:

Tagging the videos using the right keywords – For instance, if someone is searching for Jane Smith Nutrition Expert, your video should be tagged in this way so that it is easily searchable. You will see the tags (keywords) section when you are in edit mode after uploading your video.

Make sure that the raw file name is named using your keywords. For instance, it can read as "Jane_Smith_Nutrition_Expert.mp4", not myvideo.mp4.

Make sure the video is a minimum of 30 seconds to a maximum of 2.5 minutes, unless you have good quality material – if so, you can make your video as long as you like.

Naming your YouTube channel. Try and name it as close to your keyword choice as possible. Jane Smith Nutrition Expert, for example.

Make sure that you label everything under your name and keywords – the channel, the video file, the video title, the description, the tags – doing this will push the video up in the search results. Do not fret, even if your videos do not show on Google if someone is ONLY searching your product keyword. Your object is to make YOU and your product or just you yourself be highly searchable. Remember, you are branding yourself, not anything else.

In the image below, I show you where the raw file name is, the name of the video is, the description (with a link to your site if you chose), and the tags. They are all highlighted. You'll find this page once you upload your video. It's in the video manager.

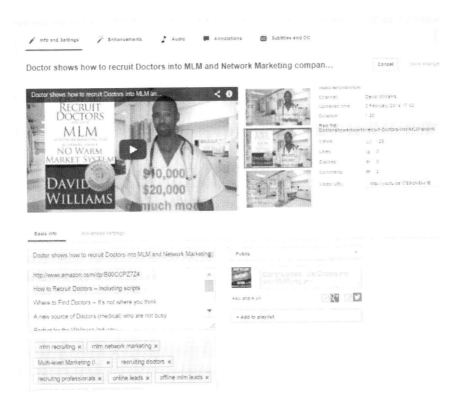

YouTube is the second largest search engine on the web (well, technically speaking, it is the largest) so you will at least create your online presence for those who are searching for videos about you.

Again, to repeat: the object of branding yourself is not to get 'leads' from thin air – you may get some– but you are building up your credibility for the leads you have, and the marketing that you will do.

Going back to the same example where you are talking to someone on Skype, speaking to them over the phone, or talking about yourself on a blog, imagine the impact you will create when you have a number of live videos. What's the first impression a person will get? "Wow! This lady knows what she's talking about!"

Setting up your videos

Setting up your YouTube videos to optimize your web presence is simple.

1. Create your YouTube account. You can have more than one account, and you can use your old account, unless it is full of non-business videos. It's best to start fresh unless you have a previous MLM series of videos – in which case you know most of what I'm covering anyway – just adjust your keywords accordingly. When you create a new account, you can add images, both for yourself and for your 'channel'. Think of your channel as a TV channel. Instead of being WKBM Boston, you create your own name. Keep it in line with what we are promoting – you as an expert. Here is an example as your username: JaneSmithWeightLossExpert or MaryEdwardsPainReliefCoach. Keep it as consistent as you can with what you have been doing from elsewhere in this book. The more sites where Google sees the same phrase 'Jane Smith Weight Loss Expert,' the better. This is why it's just fine to start small. Follow what we are teaching here and you will be found.

In your channel, you will have the opportunity to create your 'about' section. Again, this is your bio that is written to impress and has your keywords in it. See the LinkedIn chapter for your bio.

Photos – a personal photogenic picture of yourself is a must. Get a professional photo. Professional. Find a local professional photographer and get some taken. When they ask what it is for, explain you want to look like an expert, and dress accordingly. No vacation shots, family shots (unless you are a couple doing the business), and no artsy shots. Business only, not a fun image. Not 'I want to promote working from home so I want a shot at my kitchen table' – no. I can't stress this enough – get a professional head shot! FYI: don't try and crowd in your upline, or have a hat on your head with your company name on it. And smile – but not a grin. If in doubt, go to Google Images and search for the late Peter Jennings and take a look at his head shot.

As you explore your channel and what you can add there, you will learn how and where to post your expert-shot photo, as well as your channel art. If you want some nice channel sized art, go on Fiverr.com and search for 'YouTube channel art' and give the provider the image or idea you want, i.e. 'I want channel art that would look like I was an expert in health and wellness.' Have them add your tagline as text over the image, e.g. 'Jane Smith THE Weight Loss Coach.' This will cost you $5.

2. You can link to your website in the YouTube video description, and by adding tags within the video if you wish to learn how to do that. For now, all you want to do is add your videos. Generally, if you have a page that you wish people to go to, perhaps your website about you, or a capture page (where you capture someone's email address), or just your company replicated site, you should put that link first in your description. It's where people who are interested will look first. After that link, you can put a longer keyword rich message as your description.

3. Make sure to vary the description text for each video you create. As well, don't overuse your target keywords (they call it keyword stuffing), and don't use the same text on all your videos. Take the time to write up something different for each of them, but don't copy from company sites, etc., as it appears as 'spam' to Google. The time you take to do this will be worth it in the end. Remember – the best day to start this process was a year ago – the second best day to start this is today. If you can't write (be honest – lots of people can't) – take some text from your company website, 400 words or less, and hire someone on Fiverr to re-write it for you. You can polish it up yourself (editing is easier than creating), and once done, you can use this in various places. Be sure to weave your own story into this section. If any of this appears as a lot of work – it's not – it's about a day if you did it all at once.

4. Once you have your videos up, get your upline, downline, and sideline to comment on each of them, and to watch them for at least 30 seconds. This will show up as activity to Google. You can do the same for theirs later.

Other tips:

When filming yourself, consider what you are wearing. You don't have to buy new clothes, but press the ones you are going to wear. In other words, remember that people will judge you. Always dress better than your prospect. It's a fallacy that people like working with someone on 'their level' – they know 'their level' is not working and they are seeking an expert.

Second, what is behind you? Too often, I see silly, tacky things in the background – or a bookshelf of products, as if you are selling products from your bedroom. Best is nothing in the background if you don't have a 'fantastic setting.' Think about who you know that has a nice place or home office and go there for two hours – you can record many videos that are 2 minutes or less in 2 hours.

You can rent a boardroom in an office center for $40 an hour. When I would set this up for my team, we did this and operated it like a machine. It's in your interest that your team is doing what you're doing. If they live locally, you can share costs and film each other. Bring changes of shirts so they don't appear to have been filmed all in one go.

When you watch game shows on TV, each week's worth are recorded on one day, and the host changes clothes in between shows to appear different from the day before. Be a pro and appear like one.

Last cool tip:

Add music to your videos. Now some video editors will provide you with some music tracks to provide that nice level of professionalism to your project. Others don't, but it's not expensive or hard to find music.

You can get some music for free too. But usually, if you just search 'royalty free music tracks,' you'll find plenty of sites to download music from.

I find that some of the best deals come from Footagefirm.com – they sell clips of video too. You can make fantastic professional looking videos taking footage and sound from their site (it's very inexpensive) and create videos that will rival your company's produced material.

I have purchased about 100 CDs of various music and footage from them.

Why? Not for branding, but because I was tired of the poor material that comes from most (not all) corporations, and so I made my own. As long as you don't mention your company's name in the video (or trade names), or make health claims, you are usually on firm footing with your policies and procedures in terms of making your own marketing material.

I only mention this because I want you to know how powerful video is today. People like it. If you combine some voice-overs you can get done on Fiverr.com, and some stock footage and your own content, you can create some fantastic videos. Of course it's even better if you do your own voice-overs, but even so, do a few Fiverr voice-overs too. It's nice to see other people speaking about YOU as an expert. Something as simple as "… Jane Smith, Nutrition expert, recommends eating lots of kale…"

You see, your content doesn't have to be about your specific product (if you are going for nutrition expert), it can be just about nutrition.

There are also video creation programs like Animoto that will create nice looking image videos for you too. I had an outsourcer make a few for me for some of my books a few years ago. They are just picture videos with music. If you want to make a nice video of your event, Animoto is perfect for that. It comes with music so you don't have to look for your own.

Here is a link to one as an example:

https://www.youtube.com/watch?v=XDcqYyUrsZw&feature=youtu.be

Or go to YouTube and search its title: How to Recruit Doctors into or any Wellness MLM program

Once again, Google 'Sites like animoto' to get alternatives.

Want to look like a real TV channel?

Head over to Fiverr.com. Search 'video intros' and 'video exits' and you will be amazed. I would recommend not longer than 7 seconds, at best even just $5.

You can have an exciting video intro like 'More about anti-aging with Jane Smith – Longevity Specialist.' Use your keywords. Order a short one. No one will watch a 30-second intro or extro except your spouse or parents, and then only once!

While you are on Fiverr, search 'video testimonials.'

Once again, amazing! For $5 (or more) you can have all sorts of people say things about you. Now, you can't have someone make up a product testimonial (they must be true), but they can say things like "Jane Smith is an expert on Herbs... you can count on her."

Order a few of these. Once you upload them, with all your keywords, they will help fill up your page 1.

Three to 5 is enough. These are just like commercials on TV. For $5.

A Tip 'they don't want you to know about' when creating videos – save a few versions of the same video at different lengths. When you edit the video, let it run longer than the last version, and keep saving the same file so you end up with the same video saved 5 times, all a few seconds longer than each other, each with a different file name. This allows you to post the same video (but a different file name), to five different social media sites without the search engines picking up that they are the same. This will give you more links to your pages when a prospect does a secret sauce search on your keywords.

The second type of videos are the type where you 'screen record.'

Screen recording is where software records what is happening on your computer and anything you say into a mic, but you are not being filmed. In the content chapter, I'll give you ideas on how to use this.

Camtasia is the granddaddy of this type of software. It's expensive. Google 'software like Camtasia' and you can find free software or low priced software that does the same thing.

Here is one:

CamStudio: http://camstudio.org (free download)

Lets you record all screen & audio activity on your computer and create video files.

Video editing – it may sound hard, but it's dead easy.

PCs and Macs come with free video editing software – it's not only easy, but it's fun.

You have sound tracks and video tracks; once you record your video, just import the raw file, and you'll see it in the software. Hit play and you will watch your movie. You can add video in front of your raw file. You can add some in the middle, or at the end, and finally export it for YouTube. Some software will upload it to YouTube too.

You can take out parts you don't like too.

Once again, I'll tell you, if you're 21 or 70, this is not hard.

In fact, once you do this a few times, you are going to be amazed at how easy it is.

Before you think it's hard, just go to YouTube and search for 'how to edit video in – (name of software)' and you'll find 1000's of people teaching you all you need to know.

You can do this!

Now you have captured the essence of branding using YouTube. It's so simple once you get the machine started – so get started!

Final note on video cameras – you really don't need anything fancy. You can use your laptop camera or get a small one that plugs in. If you want a mic, a $10 mic will work just fine for this purpose.

Your tablet and smartphone have great video cams these days. You can get a tripod for them too – just plug in a mic to get the best audio.

Don't think of all the reasons to wait – just take action and get started. By the time you have recorded your 30th video, you can delete the first 5! The experience doing the first 5 will make you feel very confident.

Take action – do it or outsource it!

How to Mine Events for Content

This chapter is worth more than the price of this book.

This is a short chapter, but it's on its own because it's very powerful in terms of potential.

> FYI: I do mention editing videos in this chapter. Once again, I want to remind you that if you really don't want to learn how – and it's so easy – you can outsource video editing very cheaply. See the outsourcing and YouTube chapters for more details.

If you read my Mindset book, you know a lot about how I use events to learn more recruiting ideas, but there is another big secret benefit of events: the real wealth is content mining.

Just take out your mini video camera (let's face it, you can shoot a video with most phones these days, or a video camera that is good enough for YouTube can be picked up dirt cheap), and start collecting product testimonials.

Get good at interviewing people, get their permission, and start rolling. Get 50 or 100. Get more. While everyone else is gushing about the event, you get working.

Get medium head shots (close-ups) and ask people their product story. Keep it on the product, and tell people you want them to start their statement with their name, where they are from, and to say what the product did for them.

If you get someone who just says "the products are great," move on. Your job is not to teach them about testimonials; your job is to record some from folks who know how to deliver one. The more details, the better, if you hit a specific area that is gold.

For example, if you have a wellness product, and someone mentions it helped with their arthritis, you now have a video story about arthritis.

Naturally, if you are in a wellness company, people know they can't make product claims. Once again, if someone goes overboard and makes claims, you will either edit it out later or not use the tape. If you really like the story, ask them to repeat it without crossing the line. Each of you know what you can and cannot say. If in doubt, consult your upline and re-read your company's Terms and Conditions.

Even if these procedures are very tight (which is a good thing), you can still make product videos without claims. I can't tell you what to say, because it's different for each company and product. If you are really new in your company and don't know about 'product claims,' just contact a knowledgeable upline to get the story.

Get the rules. Once you know your rules, you can tape and edit your videos accordingly.

The more you have, the better. And if your company has different products, you'll find it easier to get more material for later. Remember, each story is 1 video for you.

One event can give you hundreds of 30-second to 2-minute videos if you make it your business to get them. You can post 1 new video a week or every 3 days, updating all of your social media with content.

Permission: While the camera is rolling, ask, "Can I use your testimonial on my website? Do I have your permission?" That way, you don't need to get people to sign forms, etc.

Most people, especially at events, will be so excited that they will be happy to be on camera. Others are smart and know that if their face is on the web 1 more time, that is good exposure for them. You can offer to send them the link to where you'll post the video if asked. Get each person's business card and film their card right after you finish filming them. This way, you remember who is who as you edit these later. It's always good to have a full name; getting their business card and filming it will really help you later on.

You really don't need any income testimonials.

Why?

Because you are promoting yourself as an expert in your product area, not income.

If you are promoting yourself as an 'income' expert, you will need to get testimonials from upline who will say you are a great person, but best are testimonials from your downline who will state you are a great coach, that you teach where to get leads (don't say where in the video), you show people how to get qualified, and something about how you helped them achieve something.

I won't go into much here about that, because if you are choosing to be an opportunity expert, you no doubt know what to get people to say.

Just get as many videos as possible, no matter what your expertise is.

TIP:

If you don't have access to events, go to your local meeting. If you don't have anything like that, you can hook people up on Skype and get Skype video recorder software, and record these. Yes, you can record Skype video calls! These are saved and can be edited just like videos from your camera.

You don't have to leave town – you can interview people anytime!

Think about how to do it, not why you can't.

Even More sources of Content!

I'm going to give you some more content ideas, and keep them in a semi-point form manner. Once you start thinking 'content,' you'll find you will get ideas everyplace – but I know, the first time you think about it, you'll draw a blank.

Home office tours – If you live near your home office – visit! As you read in the section on events, film these occasions and interview folks, not just those working there, but others like you who are visiting! Get someone to take a few shots of you walking around in front of the main building – you can use these shots later – dubbing over your own narration. Eventually, you will be building up a library of shots you can use. Consider how the nightly news uses shots like this of the President, the White House, etc., to over dub their own narration. It does not take much these days to look as good as the news media.

Cover each of your products – Spend some time speaking about each of your company's products, or if there are too many, talk about ones that you like or you want to specialize in. Once again, consider making many short videos – unless you really get into what you are doing and are feeling good in front of the camera – or behind it if you're narrating it.

Virtual website tour of your head office – Screen record you going through some of the home office slides from your company's website, or from still shots you have taken. Use it as the background while you talk about your company – but be sure to make notes of what you say – and relate the information that you speak about to your prospect. Here's an example:

You: "Our company is 11 years old."

Prospect thinks – 'who cares'

or:

You: "Have you ever been in a company that closed its doors? It's no fun, and that's why I love xyz company. It's been around over 11 years (don't say 11), and you'll feel right at home here…"

PowerPoint Slides – screen record – Once again, you can often get slides from your upline, or you may have them already – if you don't, then ask. In any company, SOMEBODY has made PowerPoint or Keynote slides! Often they made them and never used them. Some companies do lots of meetings and some lots of webinars, and slides are available. If not, it's dead easy to make PowerPoint slides. If you can use a word processer, you can make PowerPoint slides.

If you don't have PowerPoint, and don't want to buy it, Google 'free alternatives to PowerPoint' and you'll find lots of free programs. If you don't know how to use PowerPoint, go to YouTube and search 'how to …' and write the area you are having challenges with.

You can also get PowerPoint templates on the web for free, or for a small cost, that have nice fancy backgrounds – but don't feel you need these.

Upline and Company 'Stars' websites – Like the company's website, your upline or 'stars' in your company will have their own sites, Facebook pages, etc. that have an abundance of material.

Newsletters – Especially in the wellness, nutritional, anti-aging and cosmetic industry – A lot of the MLM or network marketing/direct sales are wellness companies. And as such, we are typically 'alternative' to 'big pharma,' 'big food,' or 'big cosmetics' – however, you can get great ideas for content by subscribing to the enemy!

The enemy?

Industry newsletters.

For example, go to http://www.william-reed.com/ and visit their 'markets'; from there, you can visit all sorts of sites like:

http://www.foodnavigator-usa.com/ – No matter what product you sell, visit this site. See all the news about the food industry. They talk about what is hurting them (you can use that), what is booming (sometimes you can use that), about how the FDA is hurting them (think about that whenever you read about how the FDA is going after networking companies) – hey, they go after everyone – it's fascinating.

I set up a leader in a networking company that offers a food alternative with so much information from this one site that she had content for a year.

http://www.nutraingredients-usa.com/

The above site is great for anyone whose company sells nutritionals. You'll find so much content in the enemy camp that you'll curse me for giving you this site: you can spend hours reading the daily emails full of what's going on.

http://www.naturalproductsinsider.com/

http://www.cosmeticsdesign.com/

Now, just to give you an example, here is a random article from the site above:

Estée Lauder profits down and sales forecast is cut

If your company offers cosmetics, you could blog or video record a little tidbit about how well your company is growing while traditional "dinosaur companies like Estee Lauder are forecasting less and less sales..."

That same day, there were stories about anti-aging products, and this one:

New York Senator pushes legislation to ban microbeads

If your product doesn't have 'microbeads,' you can speak about how bad they are, and how your company NEVER had them... or you as an expert could just speak out about the dangers of 'microbeads.' You see, sometimes you can create content but saying things that are NOT about your product, i.e. that your company NEVER used 'microbeads.' Once you start wearing your marketers cap, you'll see the news differently.

No matter what industry your company is in (if it's not wellness), there are lots of industry reports, newsletters, websites, and subscriptions you can get for free.

I can tell you, you'll be the only person doing this (for every 1000 people who will buy my books, only a handful will put into practice what I'm teaching you – if you're one of those who doesn't take action, you need to read my Mindset book!).

For all of these sites, go to the bottom of the page and subscribe to the daily (or weekly) content, and you'll get lots of stuff to talk about.

Remember, just look for any good news that supports your company's product, or find some negative news about the crappy vitamins they sell at the store. Speak about that, or write about that if you're blogging, Facebook posting, etc., and end the post or video about how your company only uses high-quality ingredients, etc. You know the drill!

Google Alerts – Let Google be your research partner. It's easy to get Google to search a keyword you set up and they'll send you a message each day with all the new material on the web with that keyword in it. This will give you up-to-date information to talk about – people will think you spend hours a day trolling the web looking for new material, when instead you're busy closing new business while Google minds the net for you.

Each day look at what Google sends you, and once or twice a week you will find a gem. For example, it is easy to set up Google Alerts for things both pro your product, and anti-traditional competitors. For example, if you are marketing solar panels, you can create Google Alerts for the obvious 'solar panels,' but also 'oil spills.' Think outside the box. This way, your content is more meaningful, and it can take just 10 minutes to create something from a story that Google finds for you.

Of course you don't do this daily. But when something good comes out, you now have material to blog, video, Tweet, or Facebook post about.

You can create these on ideas you like to cover. For example, if you are promoting something that will help folks stay out of the hospital, create a Google Alert for Obamacare. Use the keywords that you like to cover, but be creative.

How do you set up a Google Alert? By now, you know what I'm going to say – type 'how do I set up a Google Alert' into Google.

By doing the above activities, you will not only find out the latest buzz in your industry, but you will also be aware of the latest developments in your market. This information is actually more useful as a closing tool. When you are closing someone to work with you, or even closing a downline's prospect, by speaking about the industry, you show yourself as a professional who knows WHY your company is the place to be. This is far better than sounding like another network marketing 'cheerleader.'

Company personalities or Ambassadors – Most companies have one or two corporate folks who are passionate about their products and give and give and give. Sometimes it's the company president, sometimes it's a 'science officer' or nutritional expert, inventor, discoverer, etc.

But each company has an expert. There are usually many YouTube videos, websites, and blog posts of their information. Your job is just to make a few notes – to create your bite sized sound bites of 30 seconds to 3 minutes – more if you really know your stuff and if you are a good presenter (if you are not a good presenter, stick to shorter videos until you get better – *and you will get better!*).

And do you know what? A year from now, you will be known as the company product guy or gal. A few posts a week and you will be the expert EVERYONE comes to.

Major Time Saving Tip: if you find a YouTube video filled with info and you don't want to take notes, you can subcontract note taking to some-one to create a transcript for you. Rev.com is one example that I have mentioned before, at $1 per minute. You just give them the link to the video and in a day or two you will get an MS Word doc of what was said 'word for word.'

You can now edit this into smaller sized chunks of material and put it into your own words.

60 to 75 words is about 30 seconds.

Private Label Rights Material

A note about PLR

`PLR' or Private Label Rights means that the original author/owner of a product is giving you the ownership rights to re-title it, change the content, claim yourself as the author, and resell the information.

The term PLR doesn't imply that you can do anything with it by default. All PLR material comes with Terms. These terms are the guidelines that determine its usage. Therefore, it is absolute necessity to go through the terms of a PLR before buying it. However, usually you can do anything with it.

If you Google 'MLM PLR,' you will find lots of it for sale. It's usually valueless. Most of the posts you see on the net are just PLR and that's why there is no depth or quality to them. People use them to create sites for SEO (Search Engine Optimization) reasons. They have cool titles to the posts, but once you read the article, you find it is just basic surface information.

I really dislike PLR in general. However, you can use it if you are careful. (I don't, but some good people will use it WITH other material, so I don't dis them – I just say be careful.)

Types of PLR

1. Articles: PLR articles have seen a high demand in the past few years with the increasing importance of relevant high-quality content to boost SEO rankings.

2. eBooks: PLR eBooks have been lurking around for quite some time. eBooks are fuller in nature with an average of 20 pages or so. They are mostly used by online marketers as a bonus, along with the main product.

3. Audio and video courses: you can buy these and give them away for free as ethical bribes. Sometimes there are a few good ones, and you can use them as bribes for prospects to get on your mailing list or opt-in to your lead list, but honestly, I don't recommend PLR – it's usually crap.

FYI: Amazon will ban you if you use PLR in any of their Kindle books, and Smashwords (another eBook publisher) won't allow it either.

Some people will use PLR as a guide to create their own article from (or script for videos), which is okay, if it appears to you like solid quality stuff. You just read the PLR article and re-write it in your own words, adding in information about your products or personal testimonials. If you use it like this and make sure it's strong and not crappy, go for it. But in time, you'll find that you can just create your own from the methods I've already suggested.

For example, there is a lot of PLR for 'weight loss.' For example, Google 'Weight loss PLR' and you'll find pages of it. You can buy a few articles and re-write these articles for content on your blogs, or as scripts for your YouTube videos.

Once you get started, you'll find it easy to write your own without depending on PLR, and I do recommend staying away from it. You're better than that!

Blogging is boring...

Don't let the word 'blog' throw you.

Originally, it meant 'web log,' sort of a 'dear diary.' But today, it's morphed to mean a website or web page that you continually update.

Traditional companies and online companies hire writers to 'blog' about anything related to their company, customers, clients, or industry to attract the search engines and 'eyeballs.'

For our purposes, blogging is a lot easier.

Like all the other social media posting you do, it can take on a life of its own if you feel you must keep your 'blog' updated on a regular basis.

You will not have to do that.

Remember your secret sauce keywords – include your name and expertise so your prospect is going to find your blogs, videos, images, etc. The other bloggers are relying only on a search by keyword and thus are in a very difficult positon to make it to page 1.

Don't expect to get leads from your blog. Your blog posting is only to position yourself as an expert and fill up page 1 of Google. You many get some leads from it, but that's just gravy. Having said that, be sure to put in 'work with me' links back to your lead capture page or your company's replicated recruiting site.

For our purposes, you only need a few pages written, on different dates. You can add more when you have more, but don't make it a priority.

Prospecting is your priority.

Remember, you are not expecting leads from your blogs, videos, etc. We are only building pages to fill page 1 of Google.

But what if people read my blog and see it's not 'active'?

First, 90% of people will not be 'researching you,' they will be 'scanning.' Today, this is how most of us 'read' items on the net. 'Scanners' will note your blog pages, and read a few lines here and there. Those who are in the 10%, who read each and every post and judge you by them, are not your prospects.

There is an important concept to learn in MLM recruiting:

People look for a reason to join, or an excuse to say no. If they are reading each word, they are looking for a reason to 'say no.'

Having said that, if you create lots of video and images (in bulk), you can feed them to your social media profiles weekly, and appear active. But think of that as a secondary goal.

What do you write about?

You will write something related to your niche, industry, trends, products, or services.

And blogging is free!

Refer to the content chapter to find ideas to write about. Just add in your keywords to the text, for example:

Once you start working on the different areas you've learned about from this book, you will find you have a lot of content already.

You have written a few paragraphs for your online videos (the narration), you have a few paragraphs about your products, about your company, about your home office tours, etc. You can use one of these as a full blog page.

You'll be able to use your keywords in the post and in the 'tags' section of the blog (you will find the tags section when you start blogging).

You can post videos from your YouTube account in your blog as a page on its own and add the text on that page that goes to the video. You can link each page to your online 'sign up' page that your company has, OR if you have an opt-in system you can link to that. The opt-in system is better of course, but not everyone has this. If you don't have one, email me.

If you wish, you can outsource the writing. You can always go to www.fiverr.com and get several articles written for just $5.

You can get a free blog easily. Google will offer you one, and it takes just minutes to set up. If you want more than one owned by Google, go to Google and search 'free online blogs.'

Most free blogs, like Google's, for example, will offer you the opportunity to use your own domain name. It is much better to name your blog and URL the same as your keywords, or as close as possible, for example, "Jane Smith Nutrition Expert" can be www.janesmithnutritionexpert.com if it's available. Eventually, as you earn more money, you can outsource the creation of a Wordpress blog site, and I would suggest using an email address from one of your domains, so this is what your email address would look like:

jane@janesmithnutritionalexpert.com

What would I blog about?

Take the information you have created for your videos – in the chapters where I covered 'what do I say' (content) – and use this as information you can post in your blogs. Remember, you are posting this to your

Facebook account too, so change it up – you don't want to post 'duplicate content.'

The experts say you must keep blogs and other social media 'active.'

However, I want to say again, unlike everyone else, the 'experts' are wrong for we networkers.

Unless you want to live on Facebook, LinkedIn, or on your blog (there are successful networkers who do – but that is NOT the point of this book – nor do I recommend it because it's hardly duplicable, which is the strategy of networking), just take your content and spread it around quickly, perhaps 2 to 3 hours a week max, to keep your blogs and other social media accounts 'active.' I have found outsourcers who will do this for me for $5 per hour, at 2 hours per week. Once you have the content created, they can post it to your various accounts for you each week.

Why should they do it and not you?

Well, the best reason is because they will not waste any time on those social media sites (since they are yours). The reason I pay them for 2 hours only is because I have timed how long it takes to copy and paste pre-written content, embed (add) videos to blogs, and create titles and tags. Sure, you should do it a few times to understand the process, but other than that, you are wasting time being on these sites.

Always ask yourself, "Don't I have ANY follow up calls to make?"

Otherwise, you are not working your business. The people who teach you to work on your blogs, Facebook accounts, etc. all the time are those who THINK you will get leads this way.

There are too many other ways to get leads that are much easier (and I don't mean buying them!). Remember, our point is to brand ourselves so that the prospect can find all of Google page 1 with links to us. To YOU.

If you go down the 'I must keep my social media, blogs, etc. active' road, you are going down the wrong road.

Social Media Shortcuts

Love it or hate it, social media is here to stay and is in its heyday. Facebook, Twitter, and all of the new social media platforms being released have changed our lives in tremendous ways and have made it easier than ever before to **waste time with people all over the world.**

Yes, I said waste time.

Unless you are a pro and want to recruit from LinkedIn, Facebook, etc., then don't waste your day there.

Just ask yourself:

What is the name of the highest income earner in your company?

Visit their Facebook page.

See if they hang out there all day.

If they don't, you don't need to either.

We are only using these sites to get you a full page of search results on Google.

So use the biggest – Facebook, Google+, Pinterest, LinkedIn, and Twitter. You should at minimum have these five accounts and populate them with your content updates from time to time.

Your presence on social media is non-negotiable for the secret sauce formula to work, as each platform can add a link, sometimes two or more. When a person searches for 'Jane Smith nutrition expert,' Google will show results from social media platforms.

Here, you'll find I've covered a few that I feel you must get on.

Most social media sites will allow you to submit or post a bio. You can use the bio you have created for LinkedIn, with some adjustment. Same with images – most of these allow the use of images, which you now know how to prepare. Videos too. Many of the sites below allow you to add videos; in fact, they like you using them, since videos keep eyeballs on the screen.

Lastly, there are many third-party sites that will schedule your posts for various social media sites. Read the Twitter section below for an example of this, but there are some that post to all of these sites. This way, you just add all your content into one place, set up when it gets posted, and press a button.

I'm not saying you should do this, or shouldn't. For the secret sauce system to work, you don't need a lot of posts, but posting often is good if your prospect looks at your page. Most won't. But, if you are well organized and don't get bogged down into the day-to-day posting to social media sites, but want to take your branding to the next level, a social media scheduler is smart.

Once you can afford it, an outsourcer is better.

Now, once you do find yourself with page 1 of Google filled when a prospect types out the secret sauce keywords that you have chosen, you don't have to go further.

Life is all about balance. Once your page 1 is full, spend most of your time prospecting, and hire an outsourcer to run your social media or at least use a scheduler.

Why have I spoken about making lots of images and videos?

Because it's a better use of time to create these in bulk, either yourself or by an outsourcer. And then you can drip feed the content to the hungry social media monster!

Social Media Checklist

LinkedIn page – Already covered

Facebook page – this is the one social media that I don't use – yet. It's kind of my 'final stand' against time vampires. But as you may be on it already (I expect you are), you might as well make it useful.

First, consider your images. Clean up anything that is unprofessional. It goes without saying to not have pictures of drunken escapades on these feeds. If you are over 30, you won't need this advice. Spend some time looking at your account.

Put yourself into the mind of someone you don't know, such as a prospect 'checking you out.' View the page from their point of view.

Do you have any extreme views that are better kept private? Do you have friends posting things on your page that are better left unseen?

You're in business. Take it seriously. Of course this goes for all social media, so clean up your act.

I'll cover Facebook fan pages in an email update. I don't want you to go there yet, as it's advanced and more on the recruiting side.

If you have created lots of images and videos, you can drip feed them into Facebook weekly (as well as other social media sites), but Facebook loves this sort of eye candy.

Start posting your content, and add your keywords to pages, posts, images, and videos that you post. Again, posting a few times a week is just fine. You can use lots of your bio from LinkedIn on Facebook, and the other sites below that allow you to post a bio. Some sites restrict the amount of text you can use, so edit your story accordingly.

Minimum 10 YouTube videos – covered in the YouTube chapter. Don't sweat this – make up a bunch and update your channel weekly. I'll cover some new tips and ideas in your email update, so be sure to register your book! For now, you have enough to do in the chapter on YouTube.

Pinterest account – See Chapter 20 on Pinterest and Images

Images – Besides Pinterest, there are various sites to upload the same images to – if you do 3 different image sites, that is plenty. It's easy to do more if you like. It is one of those things that does not take a lot of time and does not need to be 'active' for our secret sauce to be effective and provide you Google links on page 1. You'll get more ideas from reading the Pinterest chapter.

Google Plus account – Like Facebook, but a bit different. I do have one of these; you're welcome to search me out and be part of my circle. But I don't hang out there. You have different options than FB, and as it's owned by Google (you get a lot of link power between it, YouTube, and some of the other sites that Google owns). You can put up a lot of your videos there and 'share them' there. Of course you can do the same with images, etc. I have an outsourcer add videos, etc. to my account from time to time.

Google Blog – See the Blogging is Boring chapter – but as a reminder: Google Blogs are easy and free to do, unless you want to get your own domain, which I suggest, and that costs very little. These are just easy to fill out pages where you can post content, create titles with your keywords, tags, images, videos, etc. that will also show up when your prospect types in 'Jane Smith Nutritional Expert' or whatever your secret sauce keywords are. Again, because it's owned by Google, it carries a lot of weight.

Twitter

Twitter is pretty simple. 180 characters and it's easy to manage because you can load up your Twitter feed with quotations. You can get third-party programs that will schedule your Tweets. If you search for 'Twitter scheduler,' you'll find many free programs to do this.

BrandYourself.com

This is a nice little shortcut that is free to use, and there is a paid version. It helps to show where you are on Google, and you might as well use it. If you have time during OFF prospecting hours, play around with it – but you needn't buy into the premium version unless you want to.   It just helps you with setting up your main accounts.

SlideShare – now owned by LinkedIn, this site is pretty simple to use. If you know what PowerPoint is (if you don't have it, you can get a free alternative by Googling 'Free alternatives to PowerPoint'), you can make up a set of slides based on some of your content, adding in a testimonial or two, and upload it to Slideshare. Do a few. Most networkers have learned PowerPoint or the Apple version, Keynote, years ago to create their own set of presentation slides. You can also turn a set of Power-Point slides into a video, add a music track, and post it to video sites.

WordPress /blogs – WordPress is another free blog, but it has morphed into an entire website creation tool. It can be learned quickly, however, it's not for everyone. You can also get themes or pre-made WordPress sites that look very professional (either for free or for a few dollars). If you don't want to learn all about it, you can find plenty of outsourcers to set up your WordPress site for you.

My buddy Wayne Gerald has built a whole business around his great Wordpress site, and offers a lot of material to his team and anyone who wants to visit. http://www.mymwg.com/ There are lots of ideas and tools there, and it's well worth the visit!

One of my coaching clients built a very successful WordPress site after I told her she could learn how to in a week. It now looks great and she is one of the few who I have seen build a really great WordPress site without losing her life to it.

By using an ethical bribe, she's built a list of over 2000 prospects that she drips on weekly.

Like all other tools, don't let the tool consume you. If you hear yourself say to your team member who needs a closing 3-way call, "Sorry, I'm busy working on my blog," you must realize your blog has you in its grips.

That, of course, applies to all activities, except prospecting.

Amazon Profile page – (as a reader)

Amazon pays a lot of money to Google in advertising fees. Amazon ranks high on Google. You can buy a book, and create a profile.

Once you have logged into Amazon, you'll notice 'Your Account' near the top right of the menu bar. Click that and look down the page, until you find 'Personalization.' You can upload a picture, and 'edit' your profile. Be sure to add some good information about yourself, and your secret sauce keywords. Be sure to review books that apply to your niche (if you own them), or if you are a member of Amazon Prime you can borrow books, read them or speed read them, and create a review. In your review, sign it off as "…. So, my final word on this book is GREAT! Jane Smith Nutritional Expert."

Now if the book has ZERO relation to your niche, of course you don't do that. But if it does, you should.

If you are reading this book, go and create an honest review, and put in your secret sauce keywords. Do it for any networking book you have read. Your prospect won't be reading each of them, but they will see you are an active reader who is serious about success.

Don't miss out on this one!

Bottom line on Social Media:

There are 100's more social media sites; each may provide a place marker for you on Google's page 1.

But the ones we've spoken about get more weight from Google than these others.

Honorable Mention:

Tumblr

Power of Pinterest and Images Revealed

Do your social media images matter? Yes, folks – they do!

Video and images have almost out-placed traditional text in importance in online advertising, especially in social media. Up to 85% of people consider themselves visual learners, so people respond better to images. Pinterest has exploded and it only focuses on pictures with minimal text.

Branding and marketing can be simple if you create images and videos in bulk as we have covered. Now let's go into detail on...

Pinterest:

Personally, I have found a good source of leads from Pinterest for my newsletter. 80% of networkers are women, and about 60 to 80% of Pinterest users are women too – depending on what study you read. I want to say two things about Pinterest that can help you.

1) As I mentioned once before, before uploading an image to any site, right-click it (for PC) and look at the information you find. Note the name of the file – make it YOUR name and keywords, even if it's a picture of a water filter, a protein bar, or whatever your company makes and you're selling.

Example:

Bad: DCM187658.jpg

Good: Janesmithnutritionexperthealth.jpg

Just keep changing the word 'health' to other words so you don't use the same name for each of your images or videos.

Tag it with your name and keywords – 'Jane Smith Nutritional Expert.' Even if you were putting up a picture of MY book cover (please do!), you would be smart to download my book cover image, re-save it with a file name with your keywords, tag it with your keywords too, and then pin it.

Of course you can do that with your own face, images of you at your company head office, at conferences, with your company gurus, etc., etc. Pin these on Pinterest, your blog, re-upload your head shot for your company site with your new file name and tags, and put these images as many places as you can on the net.

This way, you will have all sorts of images pop up when someone Googles 'Jane Smith Nutritional Expert.' We spoke about this for your YouTube videos, but you do this for your images too.

This is critical! You need to fill page 1 of Google and images will take 1 or 2 slots if you have posted many, and it takes little time to create these.

If you have noticed a trend here, naming videos and naming images are very much the same. You now know the 'secret' ways SEO pros (Search Engine Optimizing Professionals) use to have lots of 'juice' on the Internet. I don't want to get into linking images to sites, because that can sometimes work, and sometimes can count against you.

But if you name all your images and videos the way I've outlined, and tagged them too, you will have done what you need to do.

On Pinterest, you need to add something to each image's description. It can be as simple as just adding this on each:

With great respect,
Jane Smith Nutritional Expert
www.JaneSmithNutritionalExpert.com

2) http://pinstamatic.com/ What else can you create that people will re-pin or re-post with your tags? It's very easy to create viral content. The site that you see here, Pinstamatic, will give you access to all sorts of great Pinterest content creations tools. You can make 'quotes' – very popular on Pinterest, or any image site – in all sorts of ways.

OKAY – Sometimes I find Pinstamatic not working, but it's up as I publish this. If it's not up, you can use tools like Shareasimage.com too.

Where do you get quotes? Just Google 'motivational quotes' for example.

BIG TIP: If you search Google for 'fitness motivational quotes,' you'll find most of these fit network marketing. 'Never stop,' 'Don't quit,' etc. Amazing! The lessons we teach in networking are valid in all areas of life. That's why I never let anyone put down our industry. Even people who walk away unhappy carry with them seeds of positive growth – and they will grow all the more for being part of us.

Steps:

Google 'Motivational Quotes' (or sales quotes, fitness quotes, attitude quotes, etc.)

Copy and Paste them into a Word document as a list.

Go to one of the sites mentioned and use one quote to create one image. You don't even need an image to create a quote, just a blank canvas.

From the steps above, take these quotes and create images.

Personally, I outsourced this work to a person in India to take images I purchased from depositphotos.com, and add quotes and my website www.davidwilliamsmlmauthor.com on them.

I hired a different outsourcer to post these images to my Pinterest page. Now when I go on Pinterest, I find my images all over that site.

Quotations (now known as 'quotes') go viral. This is one way you can get leads – even though that's not your aim – some people will visit the site you have added to the image.

For example, you could do this for anti-aging, or any other niche in MLM. You don't need to create hundreds like I did (it was pretty inexpensive to get these done in India), but do enough to make it work. I found it took little time to get an image made and uploaded to Pinterest.

Don't forget to put them on your Google plus, Facebook, Twitter, and other social media accounts too, once you have tagged them.

Now, you can't tag Pinstamatic images from their site, but you can upload them direct to Pinterest, and then download them back to your computer.

Then add the tags and rename them with your name and keywords and presto, it's now tagged and ready. Just pin it or upload it again (it's okay to repeat the photo as it has a different file name anyway).

If you don't know how to download an image, right-click it and 'save image as' to a file you have created for this purpose.

If you want something fun, you can re-create that look and feel of the British War Poster, Keep Calm and Carry On, by going to http://www.keepcalm-o-matic.co.uk/. There are a lot of these on Pinterest.

- Keep Calm and Be an Anti-Ager
- Keep Calm and take Juice Plus.
- Keep Calm and use SA8
- Keep Calm and Herbalife.
- Make up your own!

If you don't know what sites to use besides Pinterest (and your normal social media sites), you can Google 'social media photo sharing sites.'

Warning: Just don't use anyone's images without permission. You can find a lot of images you can use freely on Wikipedia, and federal US government sites. Look for 'public domain photos' on Google and you'll find many. This is another 'secret' that most people have no idea about.

Go to Google images

Search for an image

Once you are on the page with some images, in the right hand corner you'll find the 'gear' symbol

Click the gear

Go to advanced search

Go to usage rights

Select 'free to use, even commercially'

Search again, and you will find images that you can use freely, but make sure you can by looking at the site itself to double check.

Once again, there are lots of public domain photos if you search for them.

NOTE: there are lots of public domain books, and movies out there too. If you can find a use for them, go for it!

Bottom line is, create some images, all tagged and keyworded with your info, and create many if you can in bulk. They are very simple, fast, and easy to do.

You'll get a lot more ideas like this, and places to find free images if you register your book with me.

Remember:

Post all images to all of your sites (not all at once).

If you are posting yourself (and not using an outsourcer), post different images to different sites each day of the week that you do your posting.

You can save a lot of time having a 100 or so images made in advance (even if you do it yourself during non-prospecting hours), and posting a few each week.

You can post one on your blog, on your Pinterest account, on your Facebook account, on LinkedIn, on Twitter, etc. Just be sure to add a sentence that incorporates your keywords. For example, if you had the following image:

Now, go to http://addtext.com/ and add some text and a web address made up of keywords. This takes about 30 seconds.

Then select download, and this is your new image:

The file was called:

addtext_com_MTkzODUyNDk3Mjg2

Change the name of the file to janesmithantiagingexpertkeepsyoulook-inggreat.jpg

Note that after you have your keywords used, you need to add something different to each file, so I added 'keeps you looking great'. You could add anything. This keeps your image names different.

Next you need to tag this image.

Here's what Microsoft suggests:

To add tags to pictures

Open the Pictures library by clicking the Start button Picture of the Start button, and then clicking Pictures.

Locate and click the picture that you want to tag.

To select multiple pictures that you want to tag the same, press and hold down the Ctrl key, and then click the pictures you want to tag the same.

In the Details pane at the bottom of the window, next to Tags, click Add a tag, type a tag name, and then click Save.

If the Details pane isn't displayed, on the toolbar, click Organize, click Layout, and then click Details pane.

Picture of details pane displaying tags for the selected picture

The Details pane displaying tags for the selected picture

Tips

In the Details pane, you can also add a title and rate the picture. You can rate pictures with one-star to five-star ratings.

You might want to add tags to your pictures to identify people, the location, or the event shown in the picture.

You can add multiple tags to a picture. To separate tags, type a semicolon (;) between each tag.

After adding a tag to a picture, the tag will be displayed next to Tags in the Details pane when you click a tagged picture.

You can also add tags when you're importing pictures from your camera.

-END-

Apple users can Google search the same question.

Brand yourself as an Author

This may seem like a big step, but it's not. I debated adding this chapter to the book, because it's not necessary to do to grab the first page of Google - but it does add a few links– so it can help.

The other advantage is that it really sends the message to your prospects that you are an expert. A book is the best 'business card' you could ever have.

Even if people don't buy your book, the fact that they can see it for sale on Amazon, iBookstore, etc. gives you great 'expert' leverage.

Still, the reason I hesitated to add this chapter was due to the scope of the project. Each of the other steps I have already covered are things you can complete yourself, in a few days.

A book, especially your first one, takes a lot more time. This branding book was to originally only include tactics that would not take long to do.

So therefore I hesitated even bringing it up. However, I shall include some ideas for you to consider here, and later address the 'how to' part in an email update.

FYI: register this book now by forwarding your email receipt to me at davidwilliamsauthor@gmail.com so you don't miss any updates.

Things to think about...

1) you don't have to write your own book if you don't want to – you can outsource all the writing and still put your name on it – it's legal and there are many books for sale by 'experts' who don't write them.

2) this is not 'vanity' publishing – where you write a book and get 20 or 200 or more copies printed – costing you a small fortune. Today, you can use different companies that are 'POD' or Print on Demand. This means you create your book – all the text, the cover, etc., and upload it to a printer who only prints a copy when you request it. If you Google POD companies or 'how do I create a POD book,' you will find more information than you need to know! My point is that it does not require you to make a major investment. You can order a few copies for yourself, and leave it at that.

3) eBooks. Your smartphone, your iPad, tablet, or computer can be used to read an eBook. You can buy books on Amazon or at the iBookstore, Nook (Barnes and Noble's site), etc. You can have your book for sale on these sites too, just like Stephen King's books. (Just like my books!)

On a note of caution:

If you have a collection of blogs published on the net already, you can't simple re-publish them on Kindle, because Amazon will not let you 'sell' something that is already free on the net. However, you could publish them in a hardcopy version – that's allowed. That would be a way for you to become published.

Amazon owns a company called CreateSpace, where you can upload your text file and some cover art, and have your 'hardcopy' book for sale on Amazon in a few days. I use this platform, but I have an outsourcer do it. However, I have done it myself a couple of times, and while it seems daunting, it's not impossible to learn.

Kindle is also Amazon's, but they will not let you re-publish material that you also publish on the net (as I mentioned, like Blog posts or LinkedIn articles). So keep that in mind before you think about re-purposing your net content on Kindle.

One of my readers is in a company that sells food products. She has a blog full of great recipes that featured healthy foods and established her as an expert. Because her blog was free, she was only able to create a 'hardcopy' POD book. But for the purposes of 'showing up as an author,' this is just perfect. She gives away her recipes on Facebook, etc., and used a few of them added together as an ethical bribe to generate leads.

Showing up as an author on the net takes work, but is simple (though not easy).

If you take advantage of outsourcers, they can make your life easier.

Which brings us to our final chapter...

Outsourcing Magic

The realm of MLM is dynamic and fast paced. Time is money, and if you can outsource a few tasks to build your presence online as an expert, you will save time and earn more money.

What is Outsourcing?

Simply put, outsourcing just means getting someone else to do something you're not able to do or willing to do. Or it can be just that they can do it cheaper than you can.

For example, a while back I needed some WordPress sites built. Everyone told me I could learn WordPress 'overnight' and I did fool around with it for a few wasted days. However, it was much faster for me to hire someone in India to copy and paste my text and images and create my WordPress pages.

He charged me $10 per page.

When you export out a job to someone else for less than it costs you to do it, you leverage your time/money.

I have used 'outsourcers' for Photoshop work (creating covers for my books), and for other image-related tasks.

Research is something else 'freelancers' can do for you (freelancer is another term for those who do this kind of work).

For example, I had a hard-copy pile of leads that I needed typed into a list to use on the computer. We scanned the hardcopy and emailed the scans to an outsourcer in Pakistan. That person did the data-entry and created our digital version of the list.

I've used freelancers from the US, Canada, UK, India, Philippines, Pakistan, and other countries as well.

Before you think of all the bad customer service reps in India – where a lot of call centers are outsourced to – there are a lot of good workers that you can use all over the world too.

Now, of course you might think 'my business is different.' This is false thinking.

Here's an example: some networkers spend a lot of time posting on Facebook, Pinterest, etc. You can outsource your social media work. Did you know that?

What about YouTube videos? Some of what you need for your YouTube videos can be outsourced. There are a lot of freelancers out there who can edit, fix, and even create YouTube videos for you. I've used lots of them.

List building:

Perhaps you sell a product that would be perfect for spa owners... instead of 'renting' a list of spa owners to send out postcards to, you could hire a freelancers to look up the names and address of spas in your state or city, and send them your direct mail postcard. If you are working nationally, then you don't have to limit yourself to your local area. This way, you own that list. Of course you could do this yourself, but your time is worth $100 per hour, and they will charge you perhaps 5 cents per contact. You can't go wrong!

It's not legal to spam people with email, but it's very legal to mail postcards to them!

Transcription Services:

Rev.com – I've already mentioned this company in the video chapter, but you can also use them to transcribe your audio dictation. You can turn your own audios into blog posts, Facebook posts, LinkedIn posts, etc.

Do you have an ethical bribe?

An ethical bribe is any free report you may offer to a lead for giving you their contact information. If you are on my newsletter list, my ethical bribe to you was 5 free autoresponder email messages. (If you are not on my list, get on it, and pick up these email messages at www.DavidWilliamsMLMAuthor.com.)

Now you can hire a freelance researcher/writer to create a 10-page 'free report' on why YOUR industry is so hot right now. You can even be listed as the author if you like. You don't have to pay an arm and a leg, nor do you have to do the writing.

What does it cost?

You decide usually. Most freelance sites (except fixed rate sites) allow you to describe the job or task, and the freelancers bid for the job. Don't pick the lowest or the highest priced offer. And look at the experience and samples of their work. Over time, you will find some lemons, but most freelancers are good value for the money. You usually get what you pay for.

How do you find freelancers?

Fixed rate sites like fiverr.com offer lots of things you can get outsourced for just a few dollars. They call a task a 'gig.' There are lots of sites like fiverr.com – how do you find them? Just search 'sites like fiverr.com' and you'll find lots of them.

Freelance.com, Elance.com, and oDesk are big, but there are many others too. Those 3 are more than enough to get you started.

How to best describe (or teach them) what to do:

The worst experiences I have had with freelancers came when I did not correctly explain what I wanted. I assumed they knew what I needed, and I learned the hard way. If you play around on those sites, read a few postings to get an idea on how to clearly explain your requests.

Get someone to read your project or task description to give you feedback until you have done this a few times.

BIG TIP!

If you have a task that you know how to do but is not something that you would expect someone else to know, a repetitive task, for example collecting names of dentists, I would recommend recording on video an example or two of you doing the task (a screen recording) and send them the link to your video. This way, they know what you want done, and you don't have to type up a long task request. They can also see how long the task takes. You can post this video as 'unlisted' to your YouTube account, so you can provide the link to your outsourcer, but as it's unlisted, no one else can see it.

I do this; usually, it's easier for me and easier for them, and fast!

FYI: don't freelance out YOUR job!!!

I have seen ads like this too: "We'll build your downline for you, follow up on your leads, make your calls, etc." This is bull-*%&.

It doesn't work.

Ever.

Final Thoughts

1) Register the book – I'll be sending you updates, ideas and time-savers that will make the process of Branding yourself easier and easier as these tools become available.

2) You'll be invited to webinars where I'll show you how to do some of the more complex tasks – if you feel you need that help

3) Anything you don't know how to do – Google it first – if you can't figure it out – send me an email.

4) Get started. It always seems like a lot of work at first. At least it did to me. But once I did a couple of videos, or images, and figured it out, I outsourced it. Bulk production is another way to save time.

5) Think Big. Brand yourself. Don't wait. Don't think you're not good enough. You are. I'll bet you're better than 85% of the so called 'experts' out there.

6) Keep in touch with me. Read my newsletter, ask me questions. Send me an email and tell me what company you're with, and where you live. Be proactive.

7) Last year, only 6% of sales were ONLINE. Yes, only 6%. You and I are in the people business. People still want to buy from people. Don't look at the web and buy into the lie that 'online marketing' is bigger than face to face.

Brand yourself online, follow up with online tools, use webinars, but don't forget this is a people business. Pick up the phone, make a call. Get out and see someone. Get parties going – my buddy Craig Peloquin, VP of Sales and Marketing with Glissandra was telling me how important their 'wine and wrinkles' parties were for their anti-aging message.

In other words – get yourself Branded on the Net, but DO the business–person to person.

Resources

FREE! Five PULLING Email Autoresponders!!
Sign up for my newsletter and get five MLM generic email messages!
www.DavidWilliamsMLMAuthor.com

The Fastest way to Networking Perfection: Rapid Business Hypnosis CD's and MP3 downloads. These are the ONLY Hypnosis CD's I recommend and use.

From my Desk:

Want to know the $9.99 tool that increased my production massively in one month? Sorry, but you can't buy it from me.

Now this tool has been out for just 3 years, but only a few clever networkers are sharing it with their team. However I have seen the results first hand – on myself – and my team – and I believe anyone in our industry who has not achieved their goals NEED's to use this simple, inexpensive and very effective 'unfair advantage'.

I remember just how I discovered these. It was a few years ago and I was frustrated with some negative attitudes that were showing themselves just after the 2008 crash. It was all over the TV, social media, the radio, every place you went. Times got tough and you could feel it.

I knew that no matter how strong our Mindset was, the negativity was going to attack us. And just like any army that is strong enough to withstand an attack it can still hurt!

I had an opportunity to do some consulting with a fellow who was an expert in the mind, and how to influence it by hypnosis and other techniques. I was approached to consult with the company that he chose to produce his CDs and audio downloads. They needed someone to write some advertising copy about his products for their sales page. I did not have time to take the contract, but I was totally convinced by all the science I saw.

They had titles that were about Abundance, Creating Wealth, Law of Attraction, etc. Even some about general sales. They offered me a few to try, but since I turned down their job offer, I felt better by paying for them.

I started with the Abundance and Wealth Creation hypnosis MP3s and after one week, I could 'notice' a difference.

The benefits really showed after the 4th week of use. Profound is not the word for it. I found that my production was up, and that meant more and more money. I could see the results in my bottom line - where results count!

I was also 'attracting' far better prospects, and I eliminated poor prospects faster. It was amazing. For me this was just so fantastic!

I did two things:

First I MADE (not asked) all of my team leaders to purchase their own copy, and use them.

Sure I could have copied mine – but I have learned from experience – things given for free are not used. Value must be felt by the user – and the best way to have them feel the value is for them to pay too. Don't forget this lesson.

Second I told the people behind these amazing hypnosis audios that they need to create some for the network marketing industry, and not just 'generalized' but very specific. I told them they need to deal with follow-up, 'the heavy phone syndrome', feeling negative about sales, seeking good prospects, Law of Attraction, etc. I gave them a big list!

They took my advice and set them up for sale online about 3 years ago for $39.99 for each album.

But NO! They are NOT $39.99!

I implored them to offer them on Apple and Amazon so all networkers could find them. I'm happy to say they did, (instead of their own site because they are now priced much less than $39.99). These powerful and life changing audios can be found on iTunes, Amazon MP3, Google Play, Beats Music, Spotify, Rhapsody, Emusic, & MediaNet for $9.99!

If you are in a rush, just search for "Rapid Hypnosis Success Network Marketing MP3" on Amazon or iTunes, Google Play etc. Get all 5 albums, or you can buy a few MP3s from each set for .89 cents each.

I'll give you a few links and titles – but first I just want to thank the good folks at Rapid Hypnosis Success for taking the time to research and create this program. When you hear them, you will know right away how powerful they will be for you.

These MP3's are on the iPads, iPods and other devices of not only me, but the key members of all of my teams. And while I am not 'active' anymore, I listen to at least one of them daily.

I decided it was high-time to share this secret advantage with everyone.

Sadly, I know many 'top dogs' who use these too, yet don't want anyone else to known about them. They are trapped in the 'old school' competition trap.

Ok, take a look at what you get on the first album Network Marketing Rapid Mindset Hypnosis Success - Volume 1 (There are 40 tracks on each album):

I Love Prospecting - Hypnotic Suggestions for Network Marketing Day 1
Become Persistent & Consistent - Hypnotic Suggestions for Networking Day 1
Eliminating the Fear of No's - Hypnotic Suggestions for Network Marketing Day 1
Winning Network Attitude - Hypnotic Suggestions for Network Marketing Day 1

Just go to your favorite online music story and search:

"Rapid Hypnosis Success Network Marketing"

Find and order all 5.

There are no affiliate links here – I'm giving this to you because I have really seen the positive change in – not only myself – but in entire teams, large groups, and at least one company who ordered them for each distributor.

So today, do your business a favor, invest in yourself and get a hold of this unfair advantage right now!

Books:

The Only Mindset Book You'll Ever Need for Network Marketing Success

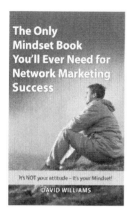

What would it be like...

To walk across the stage at your company's annual convention?
To be welcomed by your company's President as the newest top-level distributor?

How would it feel to have your spouse and family in the audience?
To never again hear "When are you going to get a real job?"
To be the leader you know you are, the example of how to be successful in this business, of finally reaching the top?

Can you achieve that?

Yes, with the right Mindset you can without any doubt.

PLEASE NOTE: This is NOT a book about 'Attitude'. This book zeroes-in on your Mindset.

Once you have your Mindset right, the Attitude will follow.
Eliminate procrastination
Keep prospecting even with 'no's'
Keep following up no matter how you feel
Have a plan to reach the top of your pay plan
and more...
If you're committed to success but not yet grasped it, it's likely that a simple Mindset correction is all you need.

Ready to change your Mindset?
Order your copy and get started today!

⏹ow to ⏹ecruit ⏹octors into your M⏹M or Network Marketing tea⏹ ⏹y showing the⏹ a NO ⏹ ar⏹ Market Syste⏹

HOW TO
PROSPECT
AND RECRUIT
USING
Postcards
FOR YOUR MLM OR
NETWORK MARKETING BUSINESS

The Low Cost Prospecting and Recruiting
Tool that Out Performs Online Methods

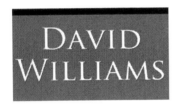

DAVID
WILLIAMS

Where to Find Doctors – It's not where you think

A new source of Doctors (medical) who are not busy

Perfect for the Wellness Industry

No buying Leads

Not working the phone

This book is going to teach you an amazing system to recruit Doctors and an amazing system for you to build a huge, profitable and unstoppable leg under them - without the Doctor using any of their warm market, 'buying leads' or touching the phone!

Full Discloser: This is a short book. It's less than 50 pages long. It contains no fluff or padding. It's direct and to the point. The system contained is worth hundreds of thousands of dollars in sales, and could retire you. Really. Forget the low price of $8.99, forget the number of pages. This book will show you a fool proof system that ANY one can follow to build an unstoppable MLM Network Marketing business by recruiting

Doctors. I have made it newbie friendly, but those with experience will take this system and put into practice very quickly.

This book will cover, step by step, and in very detailed and specific language:

The 'invisible' secret source of Doctors without a practice that are begging for something like what you will be able to show them

How to recruit busy Doctors with a practice and zero time

How to avoid the 'I don't want to go to my contacts/warm market' objection because you will be teaching them a system that requires ZERO warm market

And No 'buying leads'!

How to fill, yes FILL, meeting rooms with prospects all eager to join and try your products

NO conference calls, webinars, websites, Fanpages, autoresponders etc.

This is the full system, from the free ads you will place to the words on the marketing material you will print. This approached is very inexpensive to follow, quick and easy to implement, and very straight forward.

Also included are the phone scripts and person to person scripts you need to use when speaking to the Doctors, their receptionists, and to use in getting the appointment.

Forget all the 'usual suspects' techniques, this is not about dropping off DVDs, inviting them to conference calls, or creating special 'Doctors only' presentations. Forget all of that, and forget all of your old scripts and ads.

This system works for Doctors and requires NO Warm Market – I know I said that above, but it's very important you know this.

You don't need any paid advertising, Facebook, Internet, Twitter etc., this is all offline, local, and affordable.

No one has taught you this before. Guaranteed.

M🔲M Scri🔲t Treasury: Not Your 🔲sual Network Marketing 🔲hone Scri🔲ts

MLM SCRIPT TREASURY
NOT YOUR USUAL
NETWORK MARKETING PHONE SCRIPTS
DAVID WILLIAMS

This book is full of the top pulling, most valuable and very rare MLM phone scripts that have earned their users many hundreds of thousands of dollars. I will say right now, the material in this book is NOT 'newbie' friendly. These scripts are for pros. If you don't know what you're doing this book is not for you.

Turn your prospects voice mail into a recruiting machine! 12 scripts which you can customize

What do I say to make sure my prospects watch's my DVD or online presentation?

What is a GAP line and why you should use one, and what to say on it

How to take your prospects pulse

Top Tier Phone scripts – rare and valuable – and great to modify for your own phone scripts

What to say to get your prospect on to a conference call

How to close your prospect after a conference call – lots of trial closes, hard closes, and objection handlers

Common objections and how to turn them back into closing questions

I have chosen scripts that I know you will NOT find in other script books for sale, or the free PDFs that float all over the Internet. The scripts contained here are the kind of scripts that only the top leaders in a program have access to and it usually requires someone to be invited to join their inner team to gain access to them.

-Scripts to get a prospect to commit to a live conference call

-The hardest closing questions from the industry

-Ads that will get your Voice Mail full, and what to say on your Voice Mail screener – lots of screeners and out bound messages

-What to say to your prospect AFTER the conference call

-Voice Scripts to 'wake up the dead' – get your inactive distributors active again

-Starting your own MLM or Team Call? Need a conference call script? – 4 full conference call scripts inside

-Are you a company trainer? Do you do many trainings? Are your people dying on the phone?

If you are a trainer, a serious upline, on your way to being a player, a 'big dog', this book is for you. If you are putting together your own scripts, calls, establishing your own team, or your own network marketing company – invest in this book. Inside this book you will find: hard hitting, hard closing power calls, what to say when you reach a prospects voice mail, screeners, actual company conference calls, GAP line messages and some special bonuses to get your phone ringing plus much, much more. It's all here.

What is in this book can take a serious player to the next level.

This is most definitely an 'insider's book'.

MⓂM ⒶutoresⓅonder Messages and Network Marketing EⓂ ail Messages: Ⓕinancial Ⓦ oes Ⓟack

This book contains a professionally written email drip campaign of 30 powerful, engaging and entertaining persuasive email/autoresponder messages focused on your prospects 'Financial Woes' and how YOU can help your prospect solve them.

Warning!

If you have been in Network Marketing for any length of time, you probably have accumulated a list of prospects and their email address. However, many of these prospects have entered the 'witness protection program'. In other words, they never call back or reply to your emails. Most people forget about this list, but there is GOLD in it!

Now, you probably have an email system you pay for that is filled with 'canned' autoresponders about your company, or even some generic versions to send to your list. Some-times this is part of your 'back-office'.

But, have you read these autoresponders being sent in your name?

They're terrible!

Here's why:

You have a prospect who is looking to solve THEIR problem, which is lack of money. They need money, income, some light at the end of the tunnel, cash, maybe some dough to save their home... BUT they are NOT shopping for a MLM company, an INDUSTRY, or how long your company has been in business, or even what your product does...NO... they are desperate for a SOLUTION to their problems!

But if all the emails you send out are about 'the company, the timing, the industry...or how someone else is making money' – no wonder they don't bother responding to you!

Your prospect doesn't care about other people's wealth when THEY are broke and in financial pain. In fact, it works the other why. Resentment, suspicion, distrust.

Their mind is on their lack of money and they are worried.

They are awake all night worrying about their debt because they are in financial trouble.

And what? You send them an email about how old your company is?

It's basic marketing; offer your prospect a solution to their problem, and relate to them on their terms.

So, what is in this book? Do I teach you how to write emails? NO...NO...and NO!!!!

Is this some lessons on basic copy writing for MLM? Heck NO!!!

But let's face it. Most people can't write a note to save their lives, let alone a well-crafted email campaign. Forget learning a skill that will take you years to master – just use expert messages instead!

That's where this book of powerful 'financial woes' autoresponder messages will come to your aid.

Inside are 30 rock solid emails that focus on your prospects financial situation - with engaging humor and playfulness - showing how YOU and your program can help him out of his or her financial mess.

FULL DISCLOSURE – this is a small book – 30 powerful emails. You are not paying for the quantity of words, you are paying for the quality of the message and for getting your phone to ring.

This book contains 30 well-crafted powerfully written emails that and fun and engaging that will suggest and reinforce to your prospect that YOU are the answer to their financial problems using proven psychological and persuasion techniques.

Take these email autoresponder messages and enter them into your back-office or your email program. Start dripping on your list with these professionally written email messages – each crafted to have your prospect motivated to reach out and call YOU as an answer to their Financial Woes!

MⱭM ⱯutoresⱭonder Network Marketing EⱭ ail Messages: Ɐ ellness Nutritional Ɐack

This is a completely different set of email messages then those in the above book. You can add these to the 30 in the above book, or use them on their own. However they are written just for networkers in wellness programs.

From the Description:

This book contains a professionally written email drip campaign of 30 powerful, engaging and entertaining persuasive email/autoresponder messages focused on the wellness industry.

If your products include wellness, nutritional or related products, this drip list campaign will engage your prospect and have them calling you. These autoresponder messages contain humor, personality, and are wellness/health/nutritional related.

They are perfect for the person who appreciates wellness or nutrition as a cause AND a vehicle for profit. It assumes that your prospect likes to 'help' people and has an interest in

Interest in seeing their level of health improved.

⏃eregulation and Energy M⏃M E⏃ ail ⏃ros⏃ecting ⏃utores⏃onder Messages: for Network Marketing co⏃ ⏃anies offering Electricity or Natural ⏃as

This book contains a professionally written email drip campaign of 30 powerful, engaging and entertaining persuasive email/autoresponder messages focusing on the Energy industry.

These emails are perfect for North American Power, 5Linx, Veridian, CCM Consumer Choice Marketing, Momentis, IGNITE, Ambit, ACN - and any other energy or electricity network marketing company.

If your products include electricity, natural gas or related products, this drip list campaign will engage your prospect and have them calling you.

These autoresponder messages contain humor, personality, and are energy and deregulation related. They are perfect for the person who looking for a REAL residual income.

Each email ends with asking the prospect to call you now as the call to action.

■ ow to ■ros■ect and ■ecruit using ■ostcards for your M■M or Network Marketing Business The ■ow cost ■ros■ecting and ■ecruiting Tool that Out ■erfor■ s Online Methods

Fed up not having quality leads?

Are you in a MLM company you love, but just can't find REAL prospects to talk to?

Tried 'online' leads but found you just wasted your time and money?

Many networkers are well past the 'warm market' stage, and are struggling to find success. It seems the entire world has gone online and the problem that networkers face is sticking out in an ever increasing ocean of websites, mobile apps, opt-in forms, blog posts, Face-book Likes, YouTube movies and Tweets. It never ends.

There is alternative. There is another way.

Because the world HAS gone online, good old fashioned Direct Mail is making a come-back. Why? Because no one gets 'real' mail anymore. You have zero competition!

And what's more real than a picture postcard?

NOTE:

What This Book is NOT about: this book in no way teaches you to send those ugly, tacky, pre-printed, glossy pictures of fast expensive cars or mansions, or YELLOW 'print your own' postcards. NO, NO, NO!

If you are engaged in postcard marketing, buying glossy tacky 'in your face' MLM style postcards and mailing them out – or worse – paying to have them mailed out – I'll show you a method that will increase your success by a massive amount – because I guarantee your message will be read if you use the method I teach.

Or, if you are prospecting with one of those 'print your own' cards at the local Office Max, mailing out thousands until you're broke by sending ugly cards – you will be so happy switching to my method because it will save you time, money, you'll mail out less cards and get massive more results.

Again, because I guarantee your prospect will read your message.

I will show you a method that combines two of the most important recruiting factors for success in MLM:

Mass Recruiting and Personalization
And NO – this is not about using computer 'hand writing fonts'!!!

I'll show you a method to recruit massively with postcards, in a very personalized way for your prospect to find it impossible to not read your message and make a call.

This works. This book is based on my famous Direct Mail for Networkers seminars that were part of a $10,000 MLM insider's weekend training. You will get this same information for less than $10. And the best part of it is, this system works even better today than before! Why? Because the power of a postcard, personalized, is stronger today in this Internet age.

Full Disclosure: This is a short, to the point book. It's not full of padding or fluff, (however, I do trace for you how I discovered my introduction into Direct Mail for MLM Recruiting by a presidential fundraiser).

It's a 'How To' book. You are paying for the system, the magic, and the fact that you won't need any other information to get started.

I have included low or no budget methods as well.

Please NOTE: This book is for MLM or Network Marketing recruiting – it's not about post-card 'marketing' for non-MLM business. The information here is for network marketers who want to build downlines and offer a system to their team that does not rely on 'buying leads' from the internet and telemarketing 'survey leads', 'real time leads', 'fresh leads', or any of the other scammy descriptions of absolutely terrible leads for sale by lead companies.

Looking for a Low cost, but highly efficient network marketing tool way to get REAL leads? This is it.

Forget Internet leads – recruit real people, not virtual names.

Includes the way to personalize the cards, where to buy them at the best prices, how to produce them, where to get the lists to mail your cards to, as well as how to do this on a low or no budget.

You will also get a '24 hour' message to load up on your voice mail system to take all the calls you'll get from your prospects.

How to create the personalized card

Where to get your cards wholesale

What to say on the card

Where to get lists and how to deal with list brokers

Low and no budget tricks and strategies

Text for your 24 hour message your prospects calls after reading your card

If you have run out of ways of recruiting, if your upline is no help, take action yourself and invest in your business by using this book on how to recruit and build a team with post-cards.

This system works in USA, Canada and Europe – I know because I have used it in each of those countries and built huge downlines in this way.

M𝟤M and Network Marketing 𝟤rofessionals guide to 𝟤ecruiting 𝟤 ellness: and 𝟤olistic 𝟤ractitioners for 𝟤𝟤𝟤𝟤 The 𝟤 ellness 𝟤ndustry 𝟤 and𝟤ook for E𝟤𝟤loding your 𝟤ownline

By David Williams and Max Hailey

This book was written for you because you need to learn how to take advantage of 2015 - two years where there will be a MAJOR jump forward in the Wellness MLM industry.

Miss these steps and you will regret it. Check out just some of the Table of Contents:

Who and How to Recruit How to Brand yourself on the net Holistic Wellness:

The new Holy Grail Recruiting ground - if you do it right How to turn this 'Holistic' trend into a downline exploding movement

Wellness: The answer to the Health Crisis and an Engine for Income behind Network

Marketing Sharing of Wellness: Why Network Marketing The REAL reasons why Wellness has Become More Profitable for the Networker

How to create a Product Zealot

How to use the Increase of Baby Boomers and Active Older Adults to light a fire in your recruiting

Where to find Boomers Targeting the Fitness and Weight Loss Market 9 Reasons

Why Obesity will fatten your bank account

Why Leading with the Product is Insanely Bad advice

The 2 Words That Will Make Wealth for the Network Marketer

The 9 Key Wellness categories - Where is the money for Networkers

And much more...

The Big Money One of most important (and in turn, one of the most profitable) industries in the United States today is the wellness industry. The wellness industry touches almost everyone around the world, so it's no wonder that the industry continues to grow.

This book will show you the wellness trends that you as a networker need to know, and how to take advantage of those. It will show you new and fertile recruiting grounds, as well as retail product sales markets. Included are Action Steps for 2015 listing what you need to do to develop your wellness networking business to take it to the top.

That's why you need this book.

Because what you'll learn will give you and your team more than a slight edge, you'll get a great leap forward. Because it will show you where and how to recruit in the Wellness industry. Once you understand your industry, by just using some of the facts in this book or the terminology, you'll be able to master the conversation, write effective presentations, deliver great testimonials and recruit 'up'. You'll be able to sign up wellness professionals and build a rock solid organization of real believers and not a bunch of mlm junkies.

In short, you'll find long term income and success. Imagine recruiting from people who already are pre-sold on what you do. It's like fishing from a stocked pond.

The information in this book will provide you with REAL reasons for being in the Wellness industry so you can dominate your prospecting and keep your team excited when they hit those emotional road blocks.

Recruiting: it will show you where to find prospects who are ready to start and who are already excited by wellness products. It will show you how to approach them, what to say, and the biggie, what NOT to say!

Lastly, the book will provide you with Action Steps of what to do to ride the wave of wellness.

1) Create your Internet content with information from this book to brand yourself

2) Use this information to educate & excite your prospects and new distributors

3) Find product zealots by sampling to targeted groups as shown here

4) Recruit Holistic practitioners - people already committed to Wellness

This is an invitation to wealth. You can't help but get rich if you take action now and build in 2015.

Read MLM and Network Marketing professionals guide to Recruiting Wellness and Holistic Practitioners for 2014 The Wellness Industry Handbook for Exploding your Downline

TODAY!

The Si? ?lest? Shortest? Most ?owerful M?M and Network Marketing ?ros?ect ?ontrol and ?losing ?ines and Scri?ts

Do you have trouble closing prospects? Do you feel you lose control of your prospecting and follow up calls? Do you have trouble closing strong prospects – the very ones you desperately want on your team?

Well, this book is for you. It's the lowest price but highest value book on Amazon. Why? Because this little book contains over 120 of the strongest, easiest, subtlest closing and 'keeping control' and 'taking control' over the conversation lines for network marketers.

FULL DISCLOSURE: This is a short book. This book has over 150 'lines'; mostly one line sentences. But don't be fooled by the size of the book. These are powerful closing lines to allow you to close your prospect. This is NOT a book on prospecting, recruiting or even a script book.

This is a book that should be open at your desk as you make your prospecting and follow up calls. If you find you prospect off their script (they never stay on script – only you can do that), these lines will bring you back into control.

They are subtle, but powerful. Here's some samples:

How much does it cost?

Millions of dollars not to get involved

Can you see yourself taking people through a process just like I did with you?

You can't outsource your learning

The table's set

This is thick

I'm not claiming we have an automatic system, I'm demonstrating it

Get into the game with us

Let me layout how the business will start for you

This is just a process to see if there a fit for you

This is not a pressure gig

It's just the way we do this (process)

There's no glory in paying bills

I promise I'm not going to push you, chase you or sell you

I'm not going to come back to close you, but to personalize the business for you

NOTE: with very little modification, you can use many of these lines as ad headers, email subject lines, or as smart and directed text in emails or create new phone scripts or reinvigorate old ones.

If you lose control of a conversation, or have a strong person on the line (the best kind to recruit), these 'lines' are the arrows in your quiver.

Make these lines your own. They have been collected by professionals and have earned those who have used them millions of dollars, no exaggerating, millions of dollars. Now for .99 cents they are yours.

This book of powerful network marketing closing and control lines provides you with the easiest way to sound strong on the phone. You just need to use them. You need to sound strong. Your prospect will never know what hit them until you are training them, and tell them to pick up this little book.

⁇ ⁇ortant ⁇ essage for Tea⁇ ⁇eaders:

If you would like any set of my emails personalized for your team or company, just contact me. I have a relationship with a company that will set you up. Just shoot me an email requesting more info and we can chat. This is the best way to take your team to the next level. I wish I had this kind of tool when I was active.

Davidwilliamsauthor@gmail.com

⁇⁇out the ⁇uthor

If You want to know one thing about David Williams it's this:

He believes in OFFLINE prospecting and ONLINE follow up!

David Williams has been a top earner and top performer in networking for over 25 years. He has worked all over the world building teams successfully. In the last five years he has worked with corporations to develop MLM opportunities as well as top performers to create recruiting systems for their teams.

He also delivers 'insider only' high priced seminars for 'the big dogs' on practical MLM: prospecting, recruiting and team expansion.

Prior to Networking Williams' background was a few years of university – which meant he was broke.

In 2012 he decided to put into book-form some of the trainings he has done and offer them to anyone. Typically his work spreads word-of-mouth and word-of-mouse. Williams decided to present his insiders training at price levels that are affordable via the Internet to anyone but is not trying to disrupt the high priced seminars business either. Rather he feels that his readers are new and future leaders who are not even aware of these insider events but will one day will be seated there if they follow his systems.

Williams is not actively working any MLM program but enjoys 8 different residual income sources and in multiple currencies.

His favorite MLM tips include:

Fire your Upline
Be the Upline you want
Never stop recruiting
How much money would I make today if my downline did what I did?
He hates 'fluff' training.

He writes a MLM email training letter that he sends weekly - you can sign up for it at www.DavidWilliamsMLMAuthor.com

Those who have signed up for David's newsletter my reach him via that email address.

Feel free to contact him with any question.

Made in the USA
Charleston, SC
06 January 2015